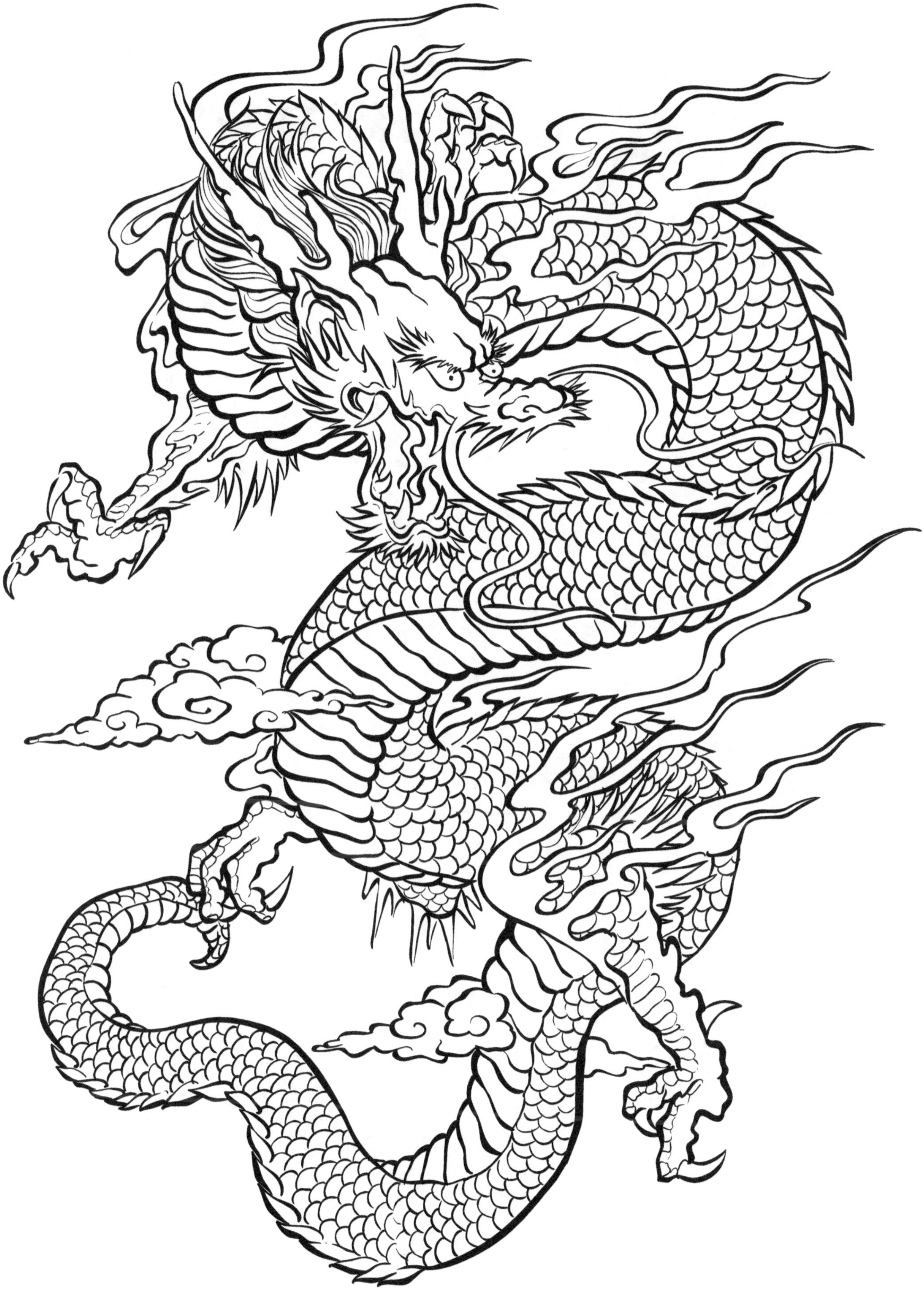

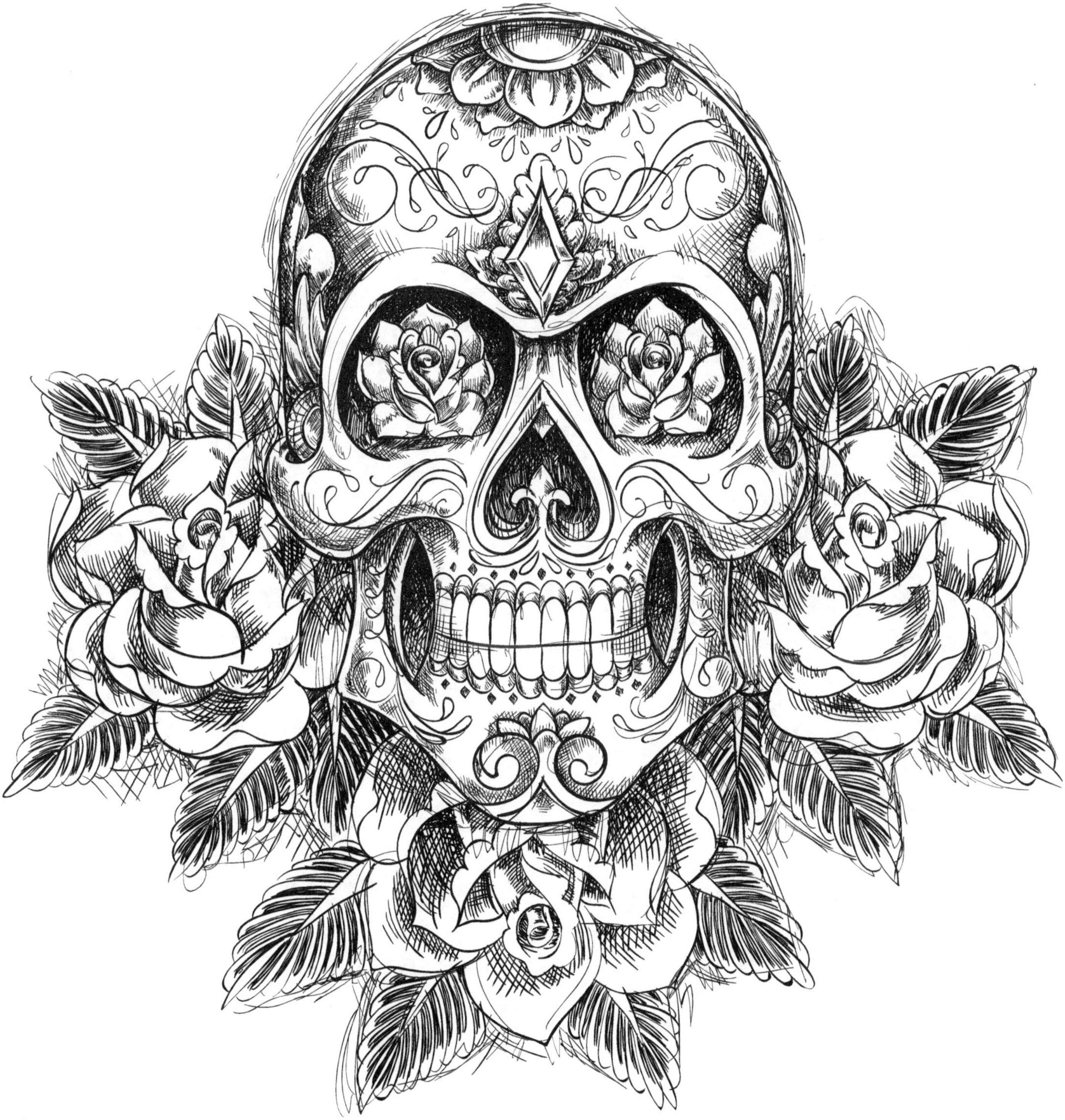

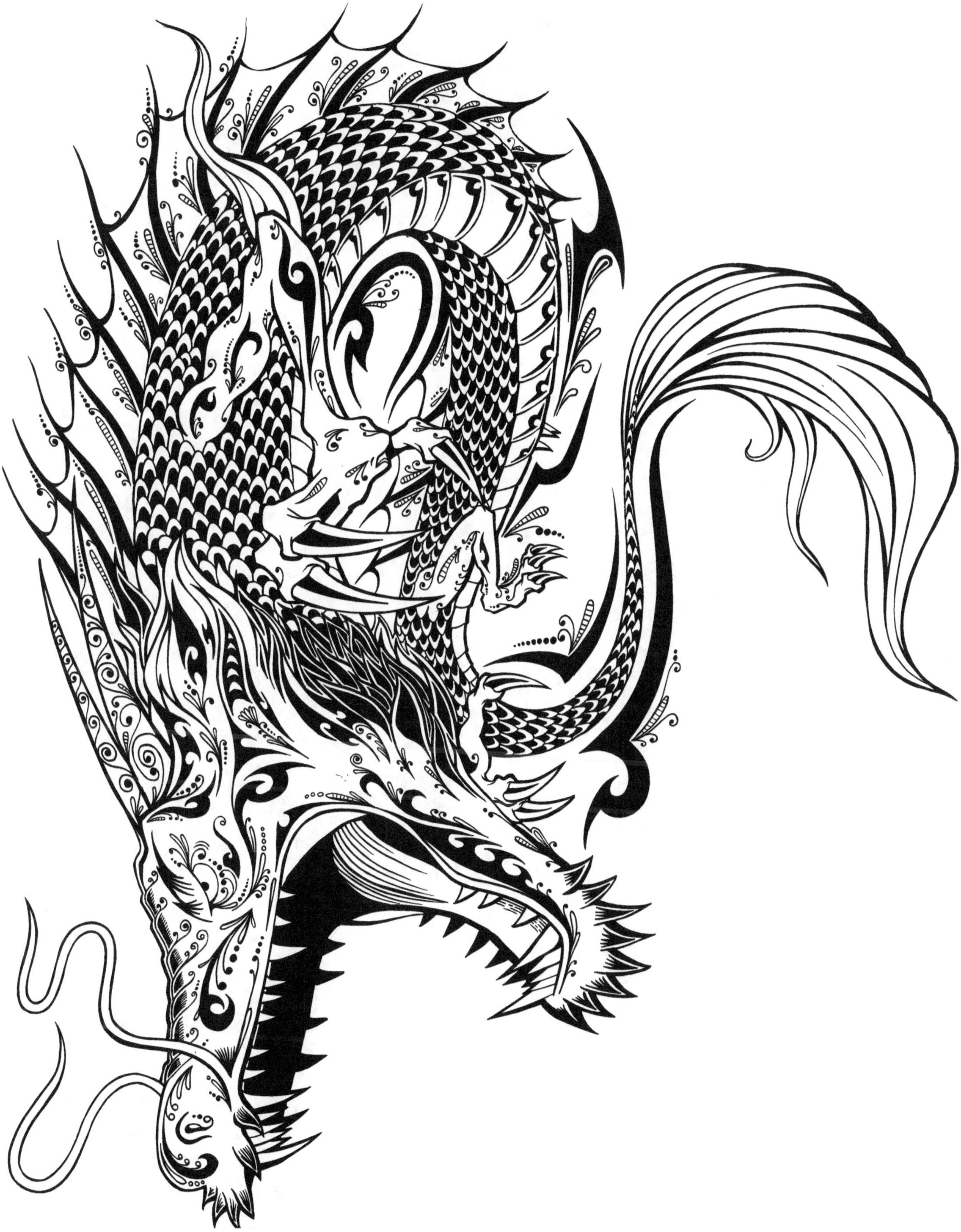

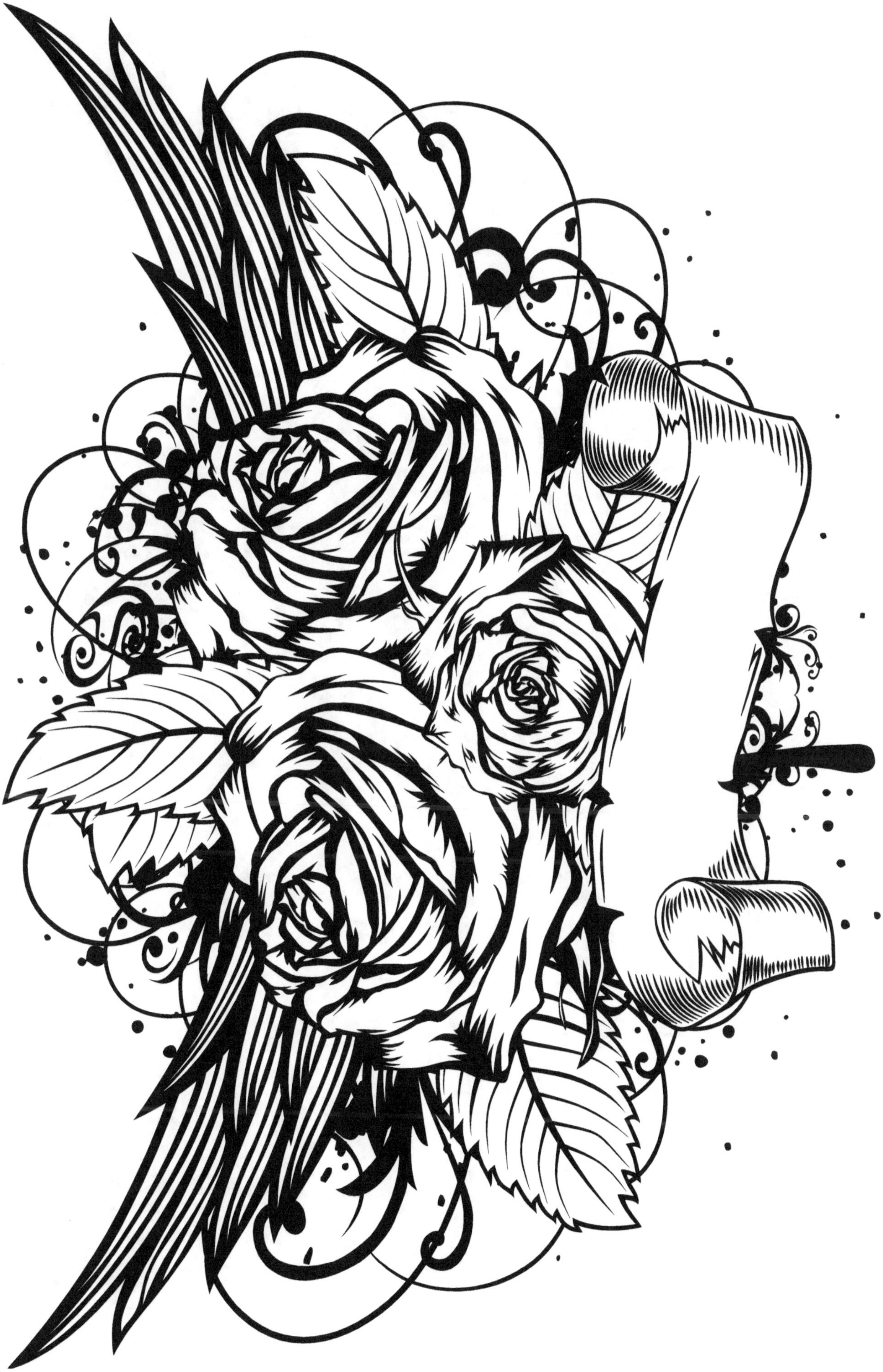

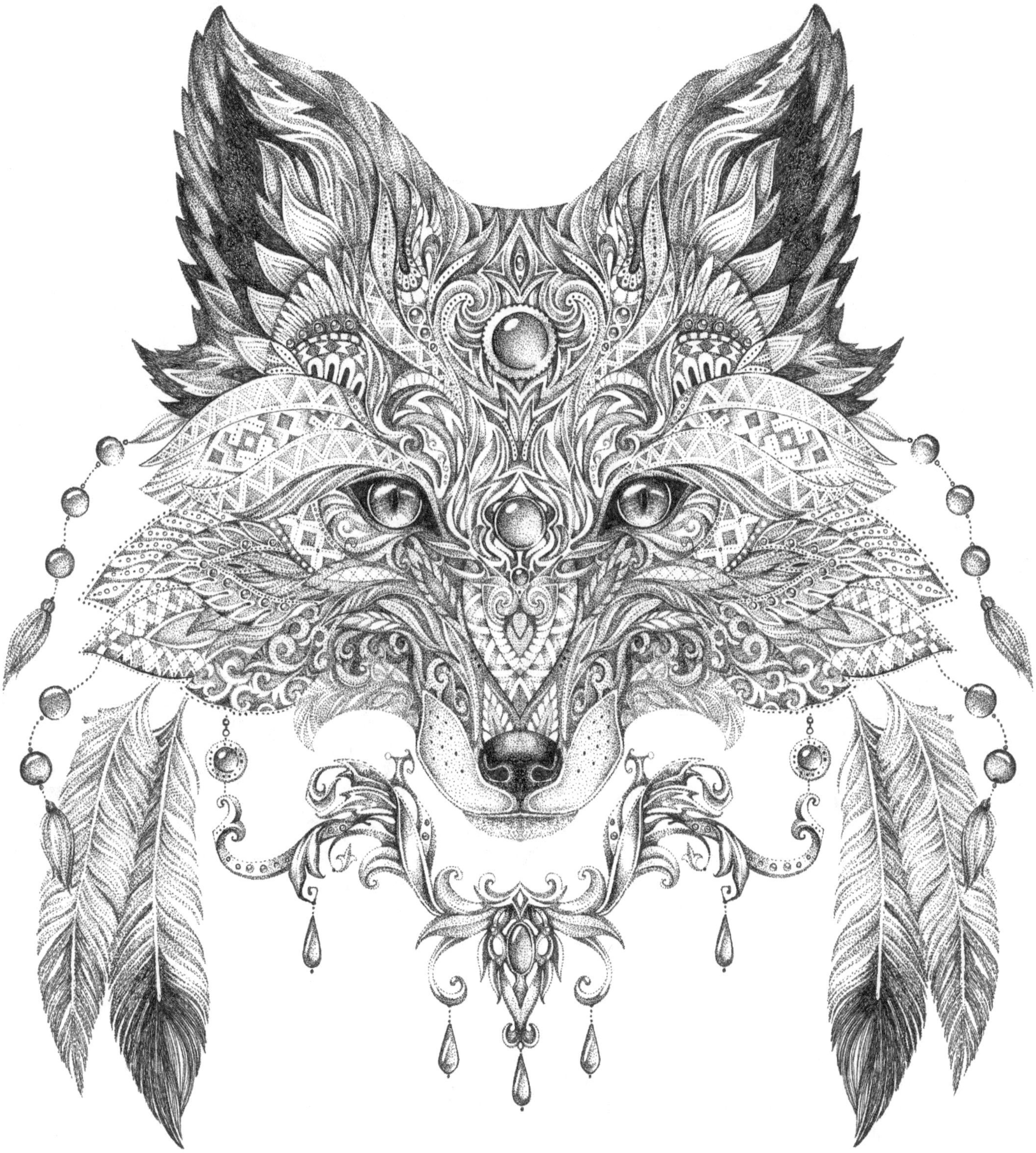

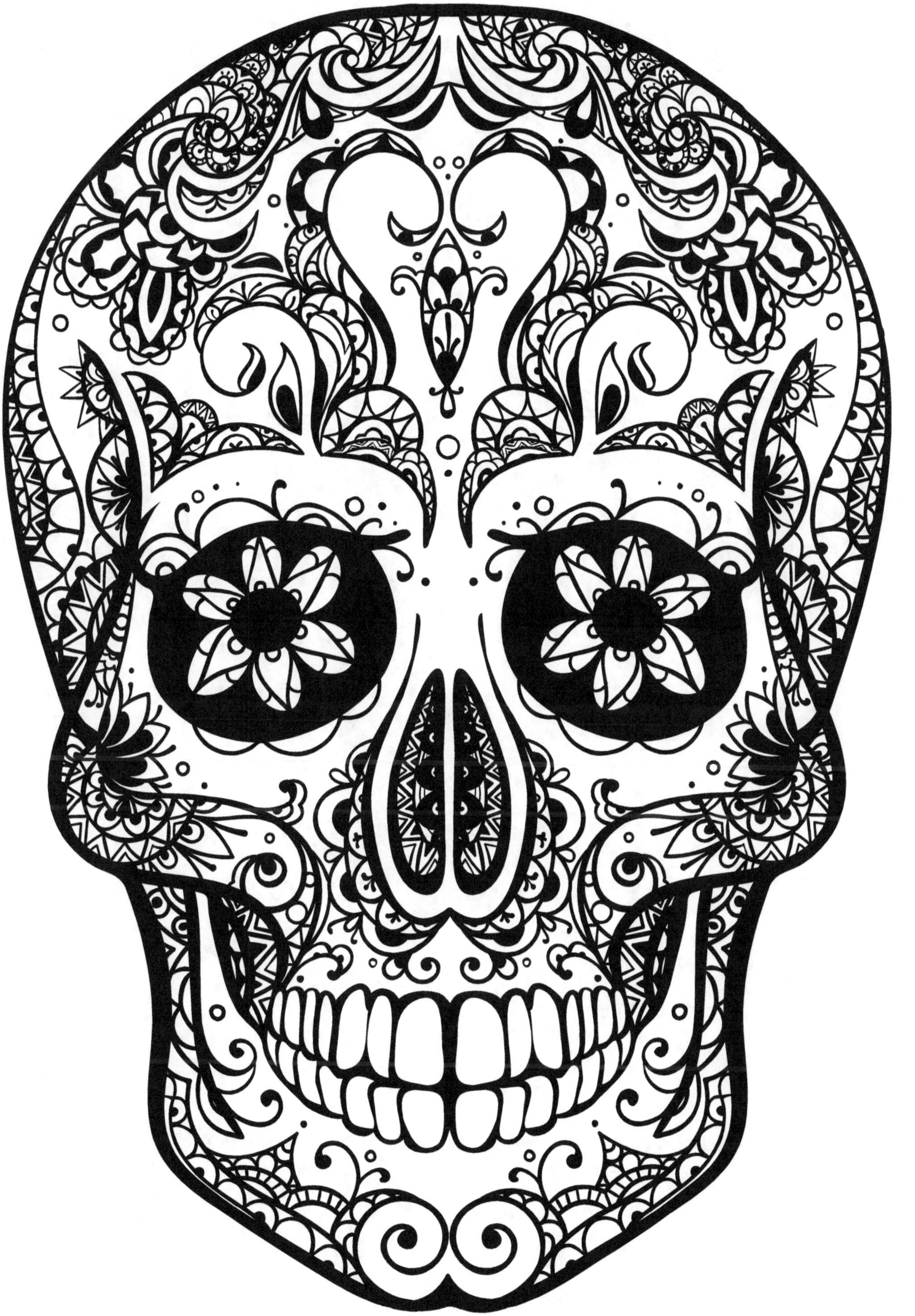

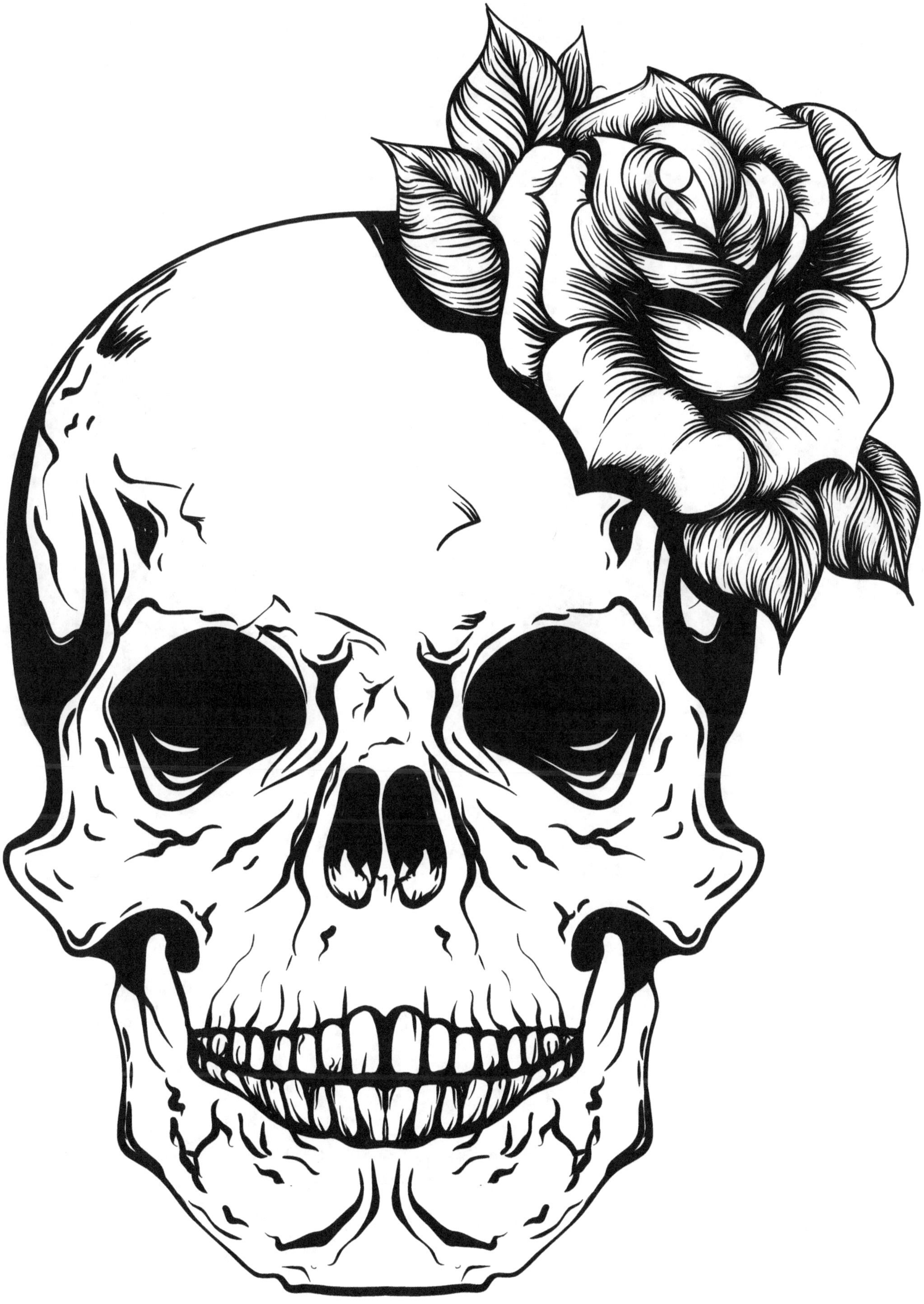

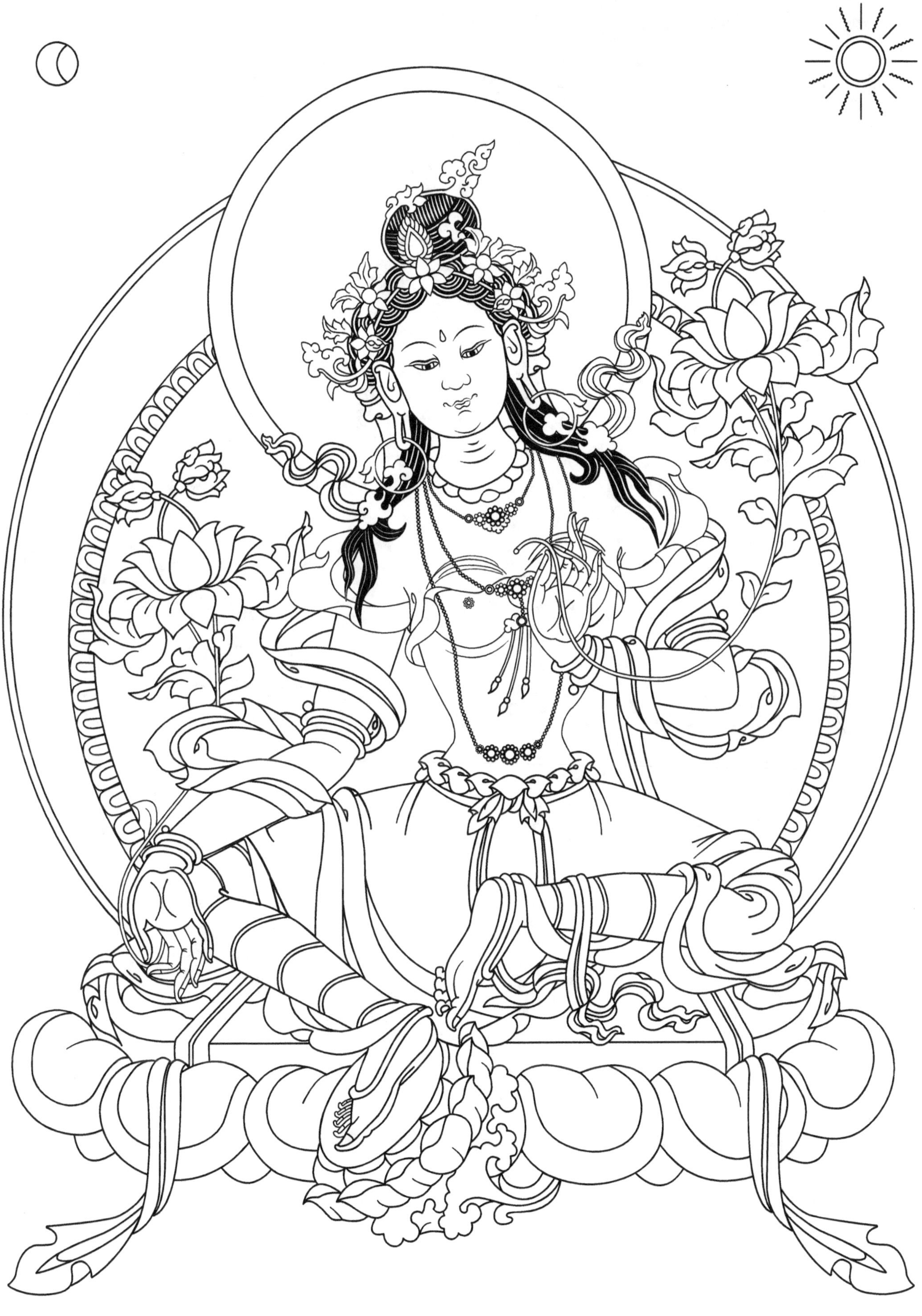

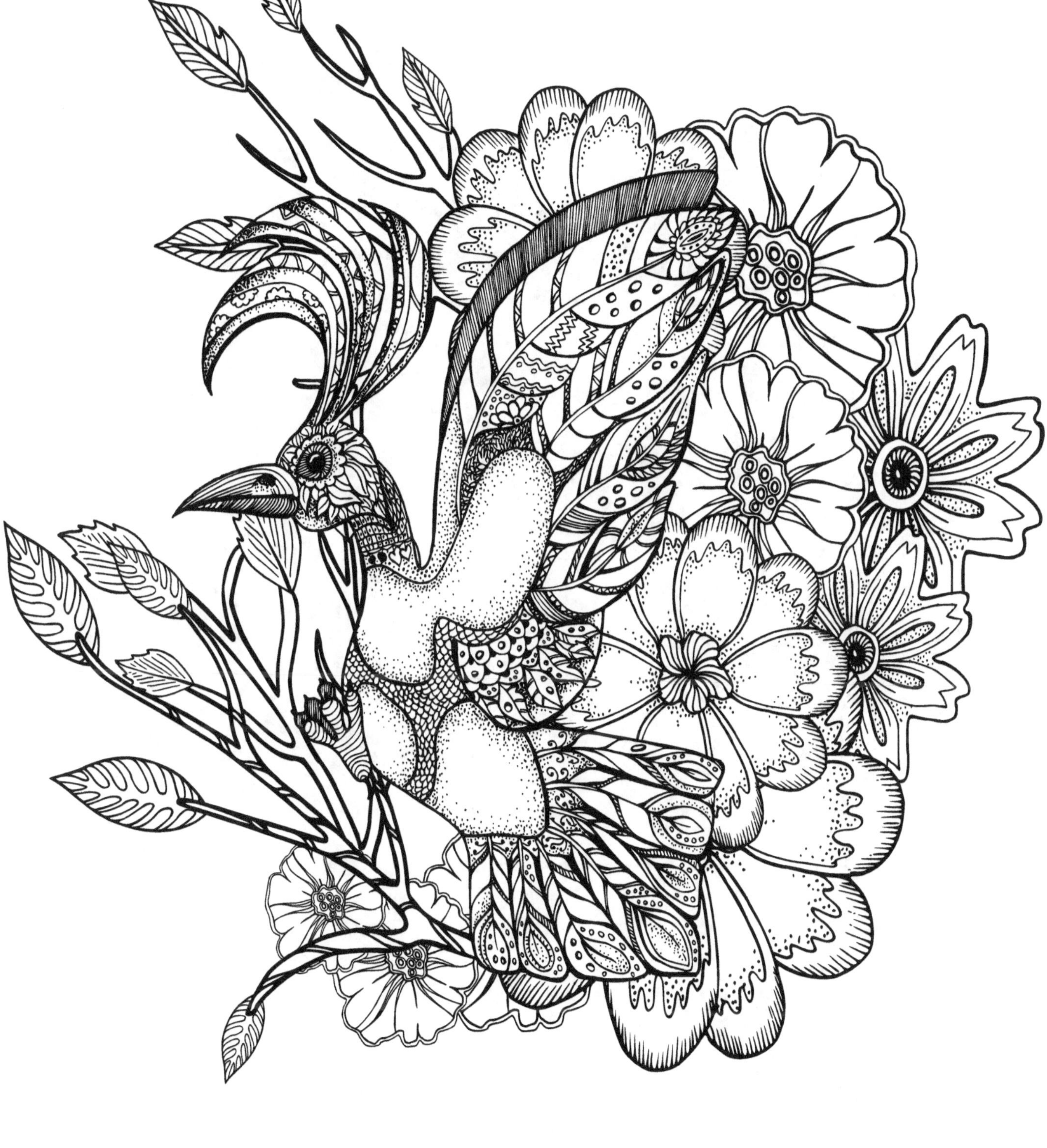

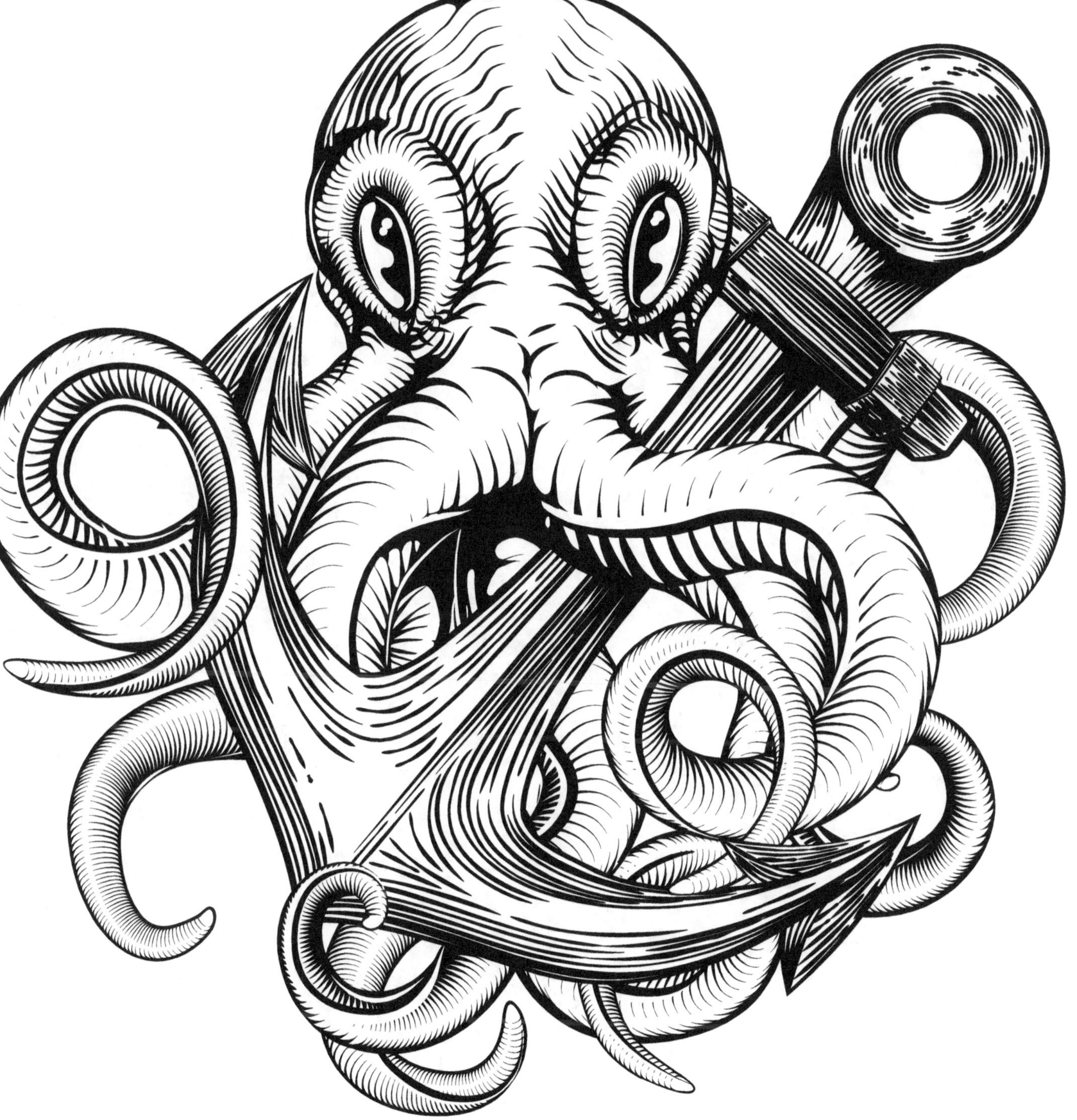

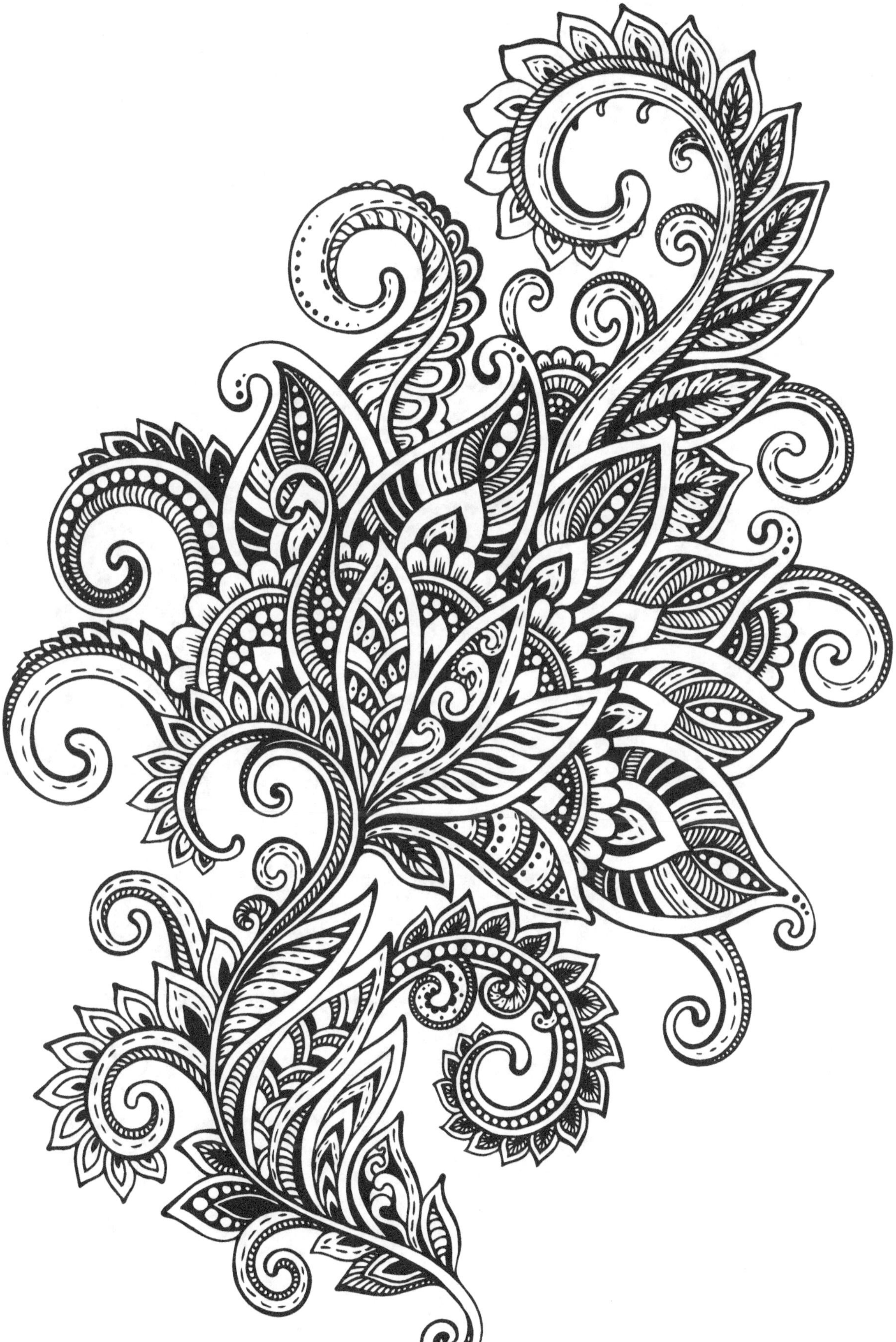

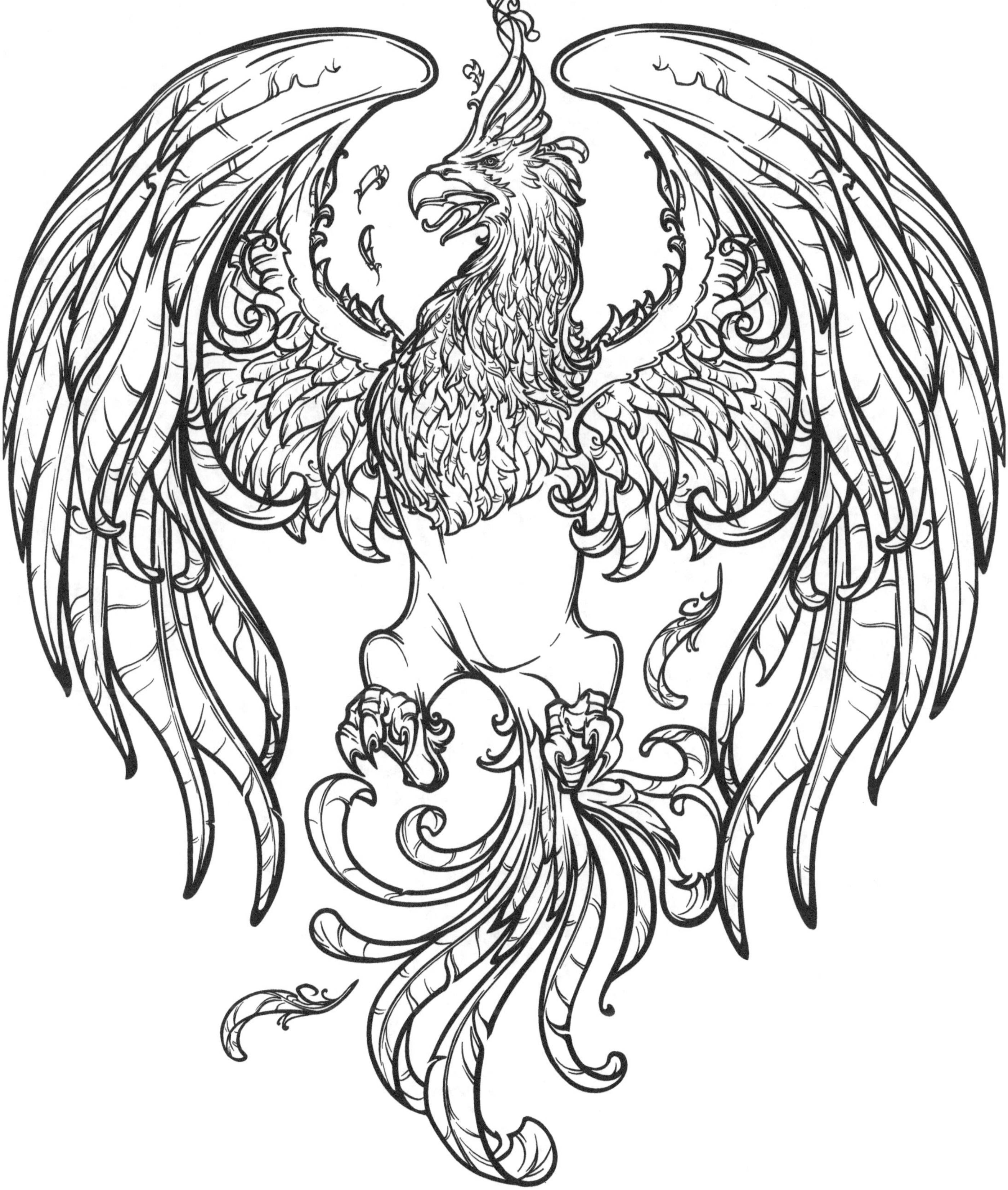

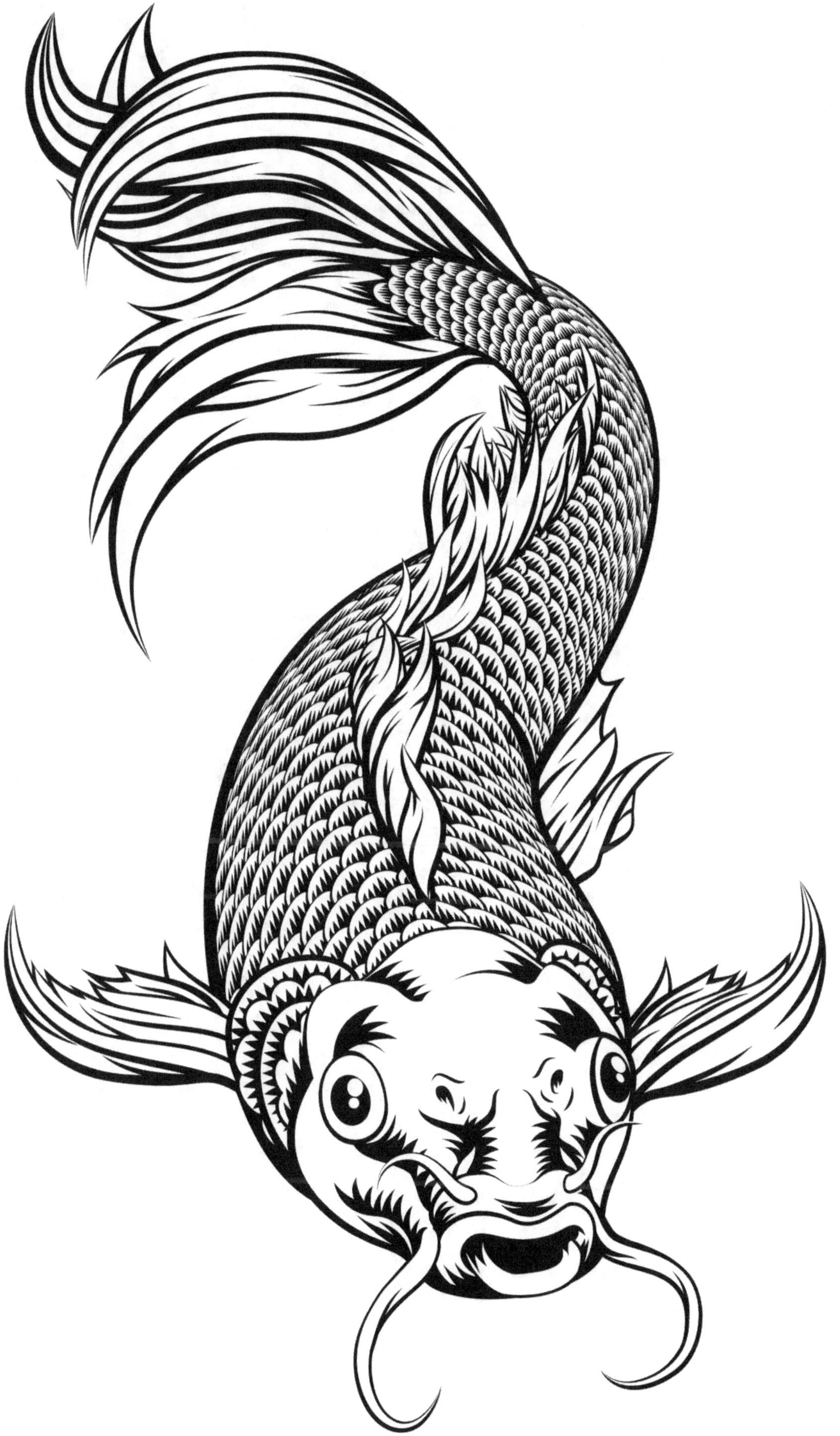

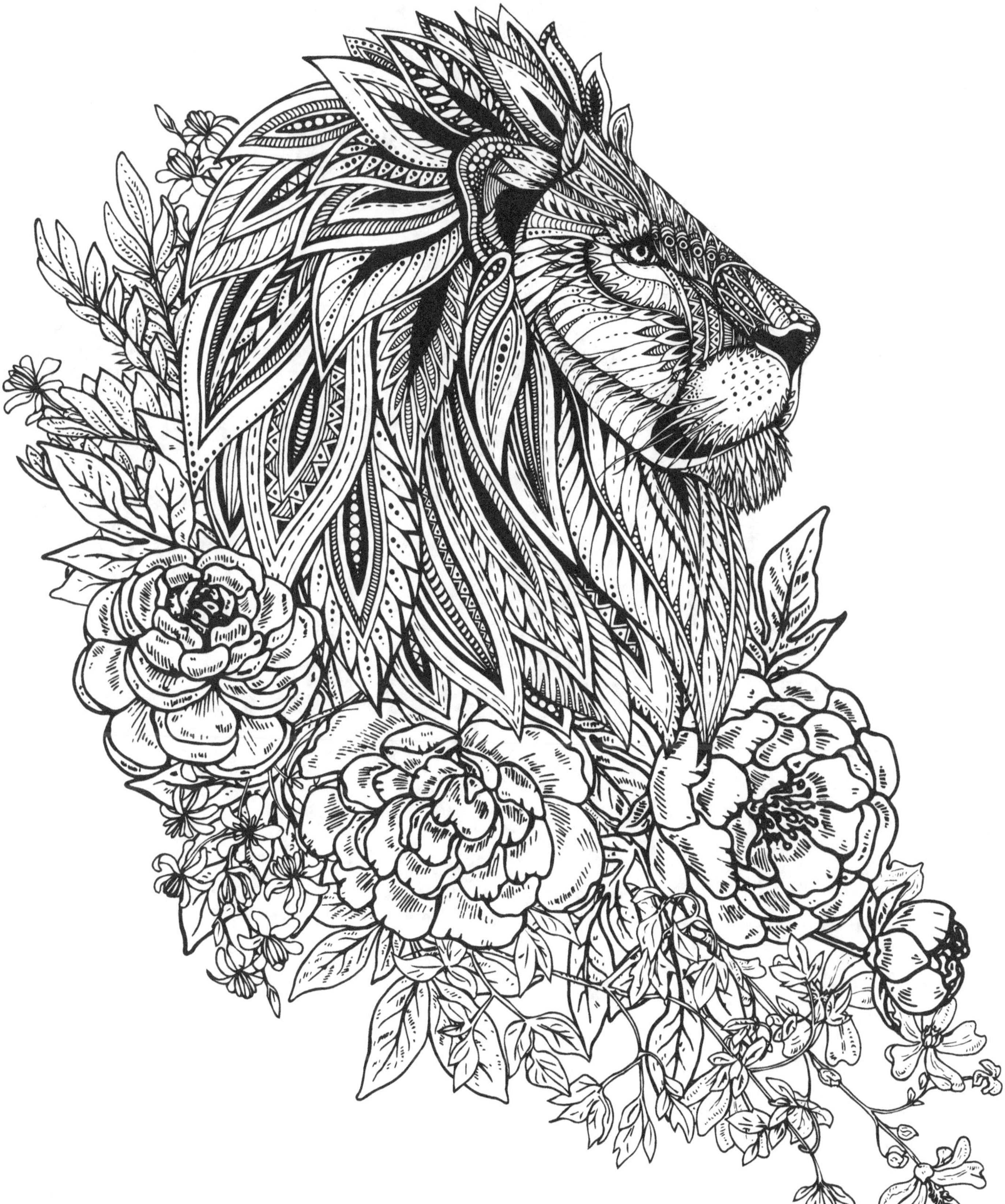

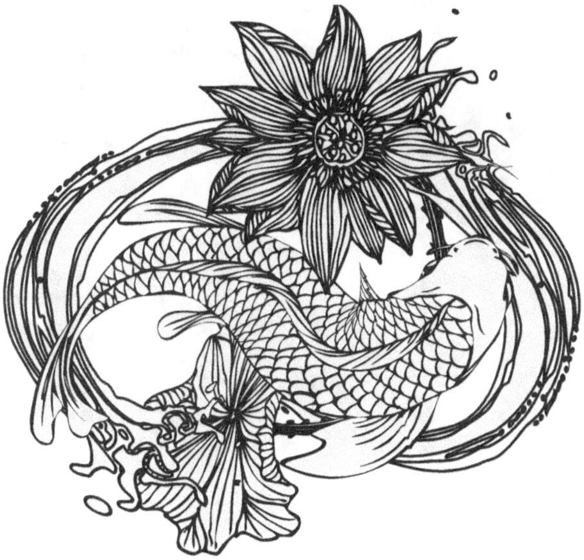
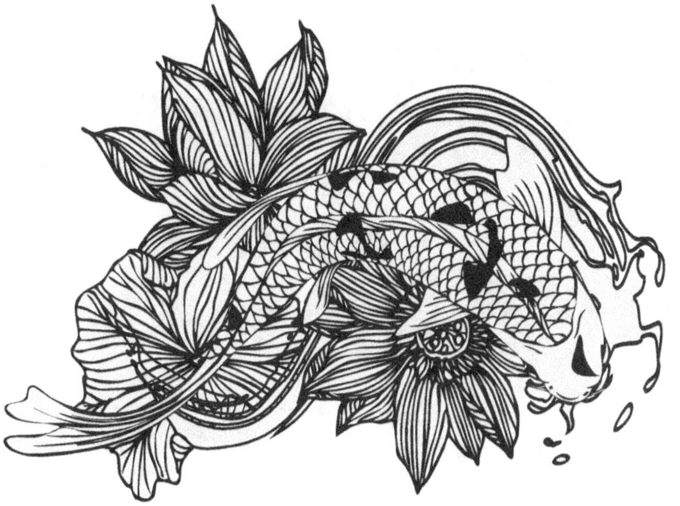
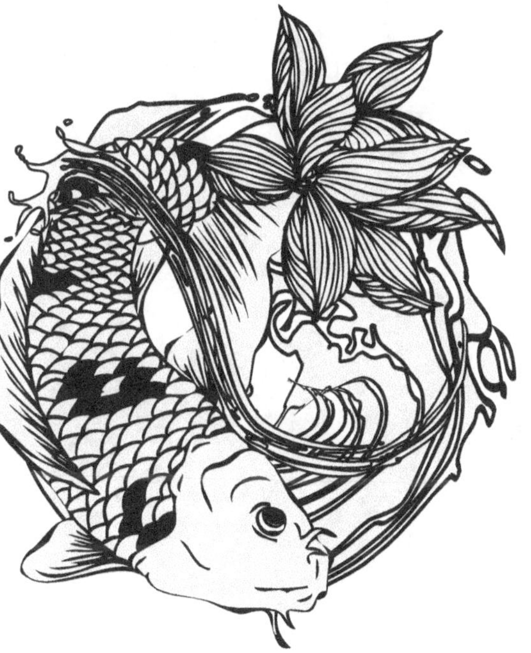
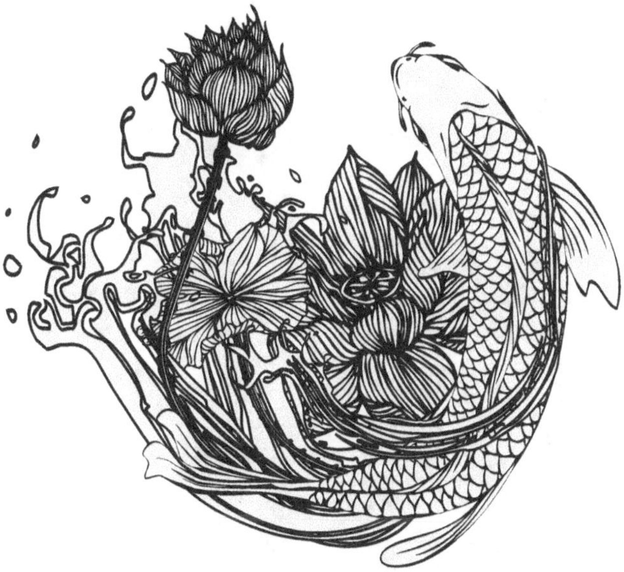
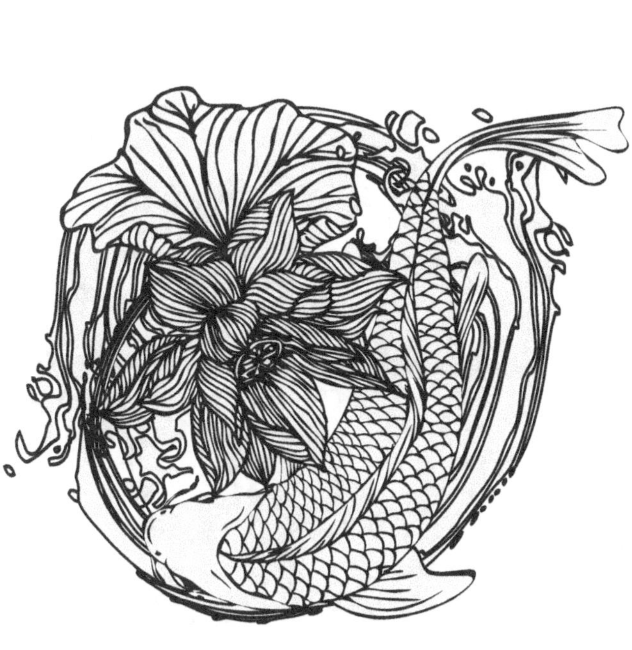
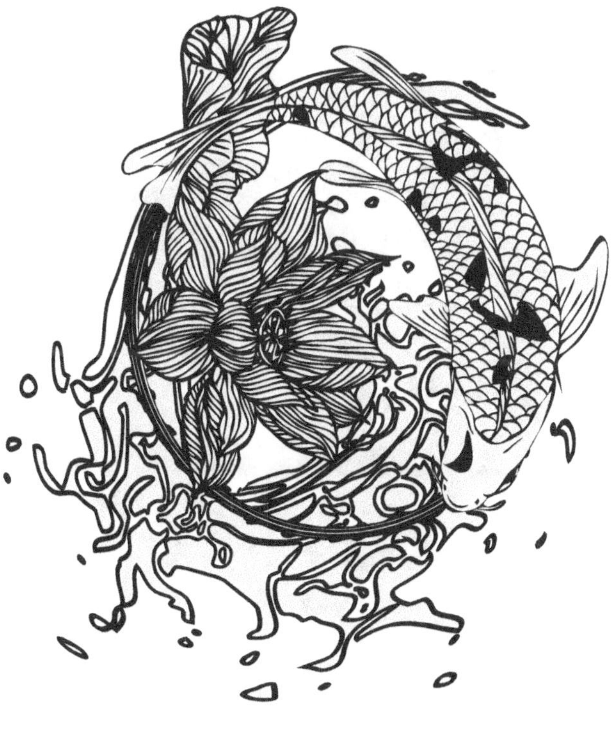

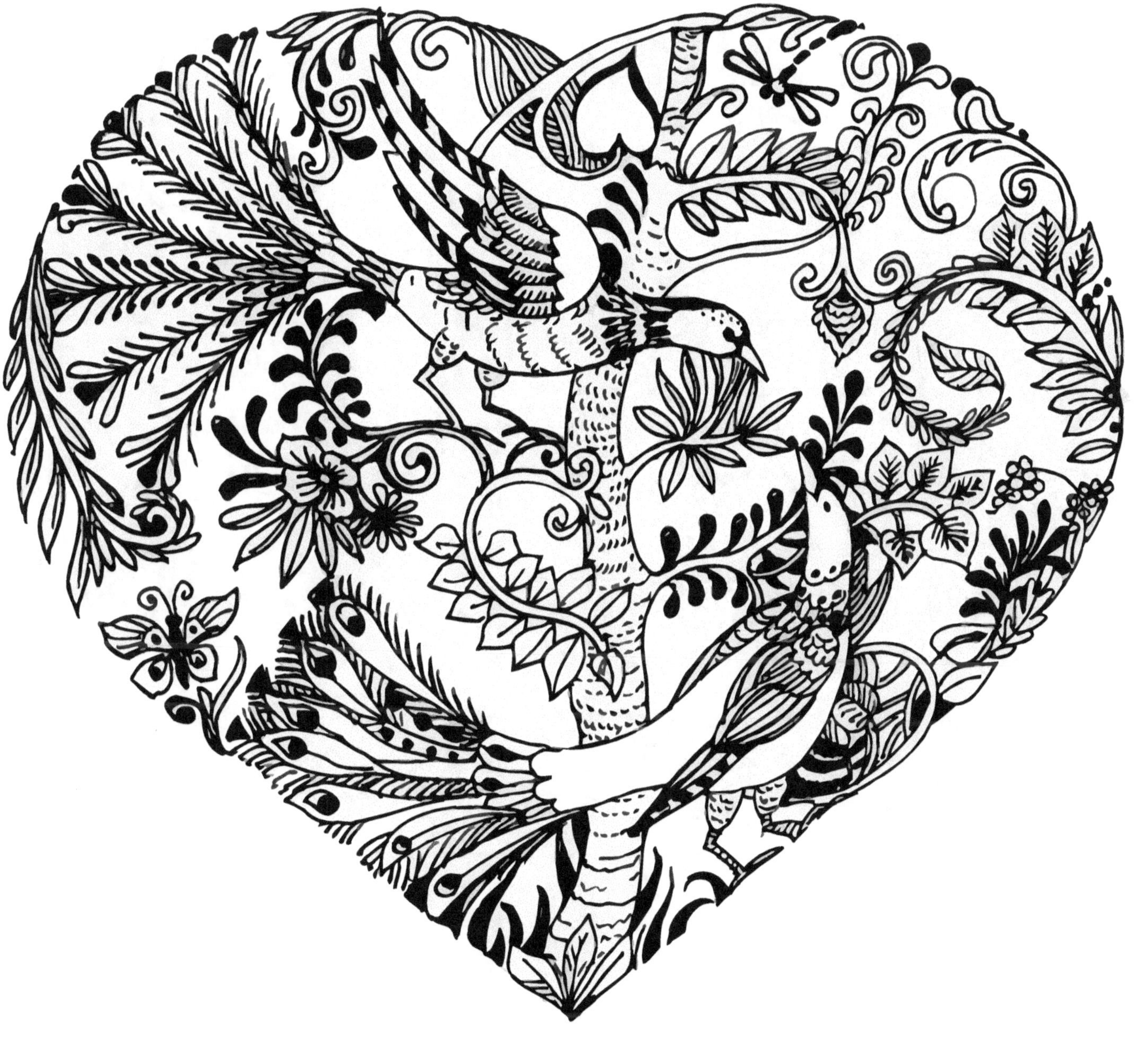

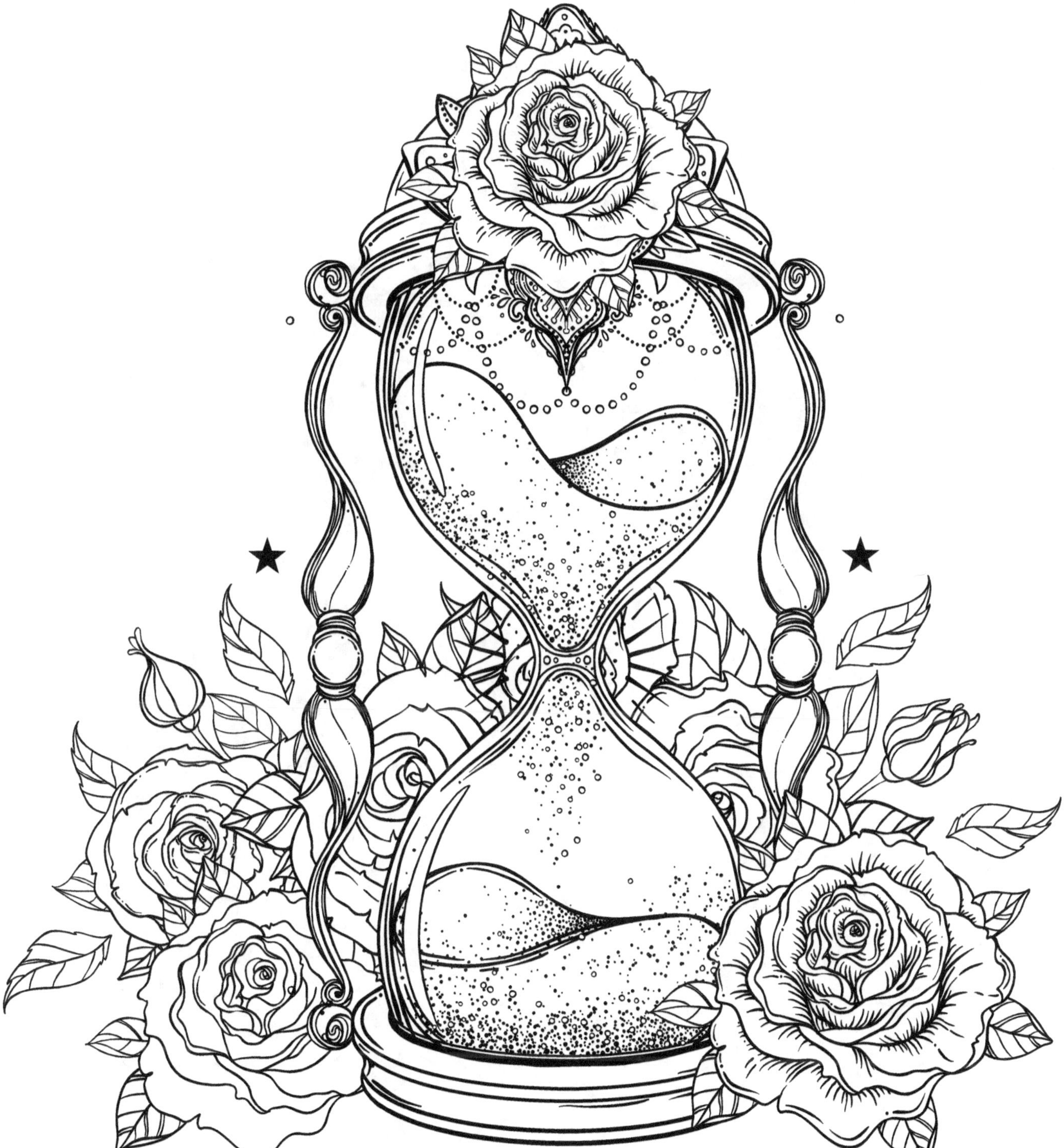

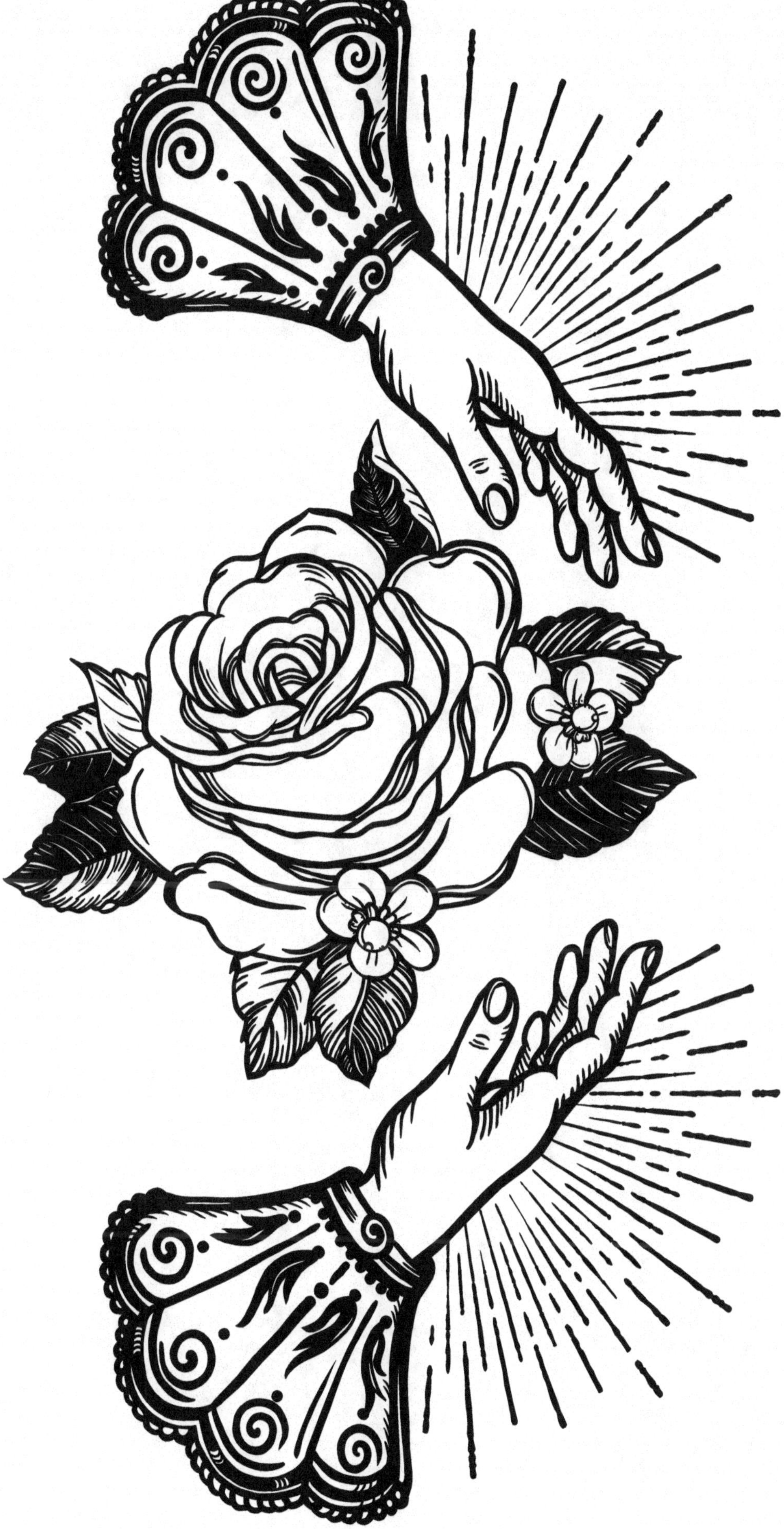

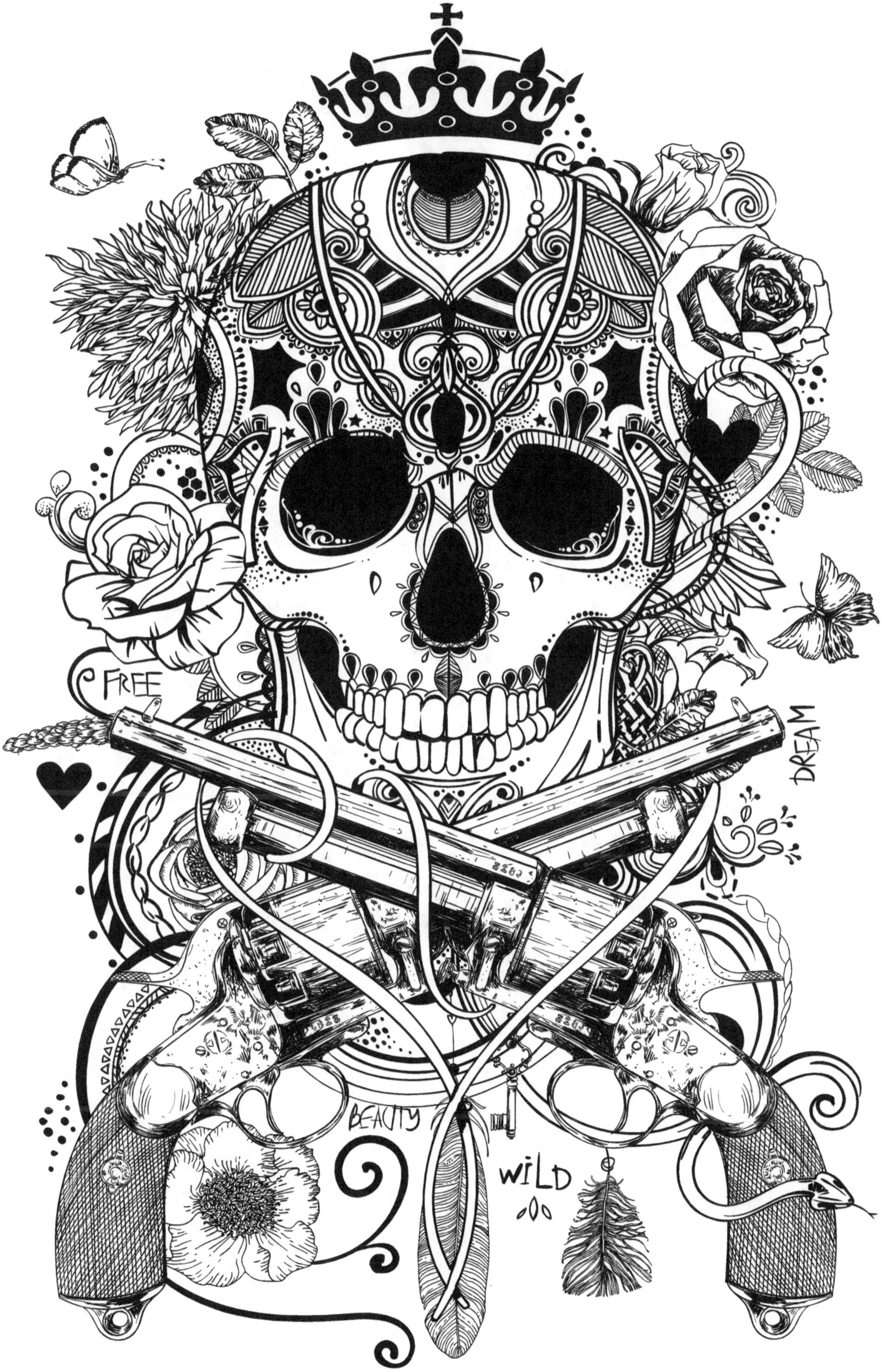
FREE
DREAM
BEAUTY
WILD

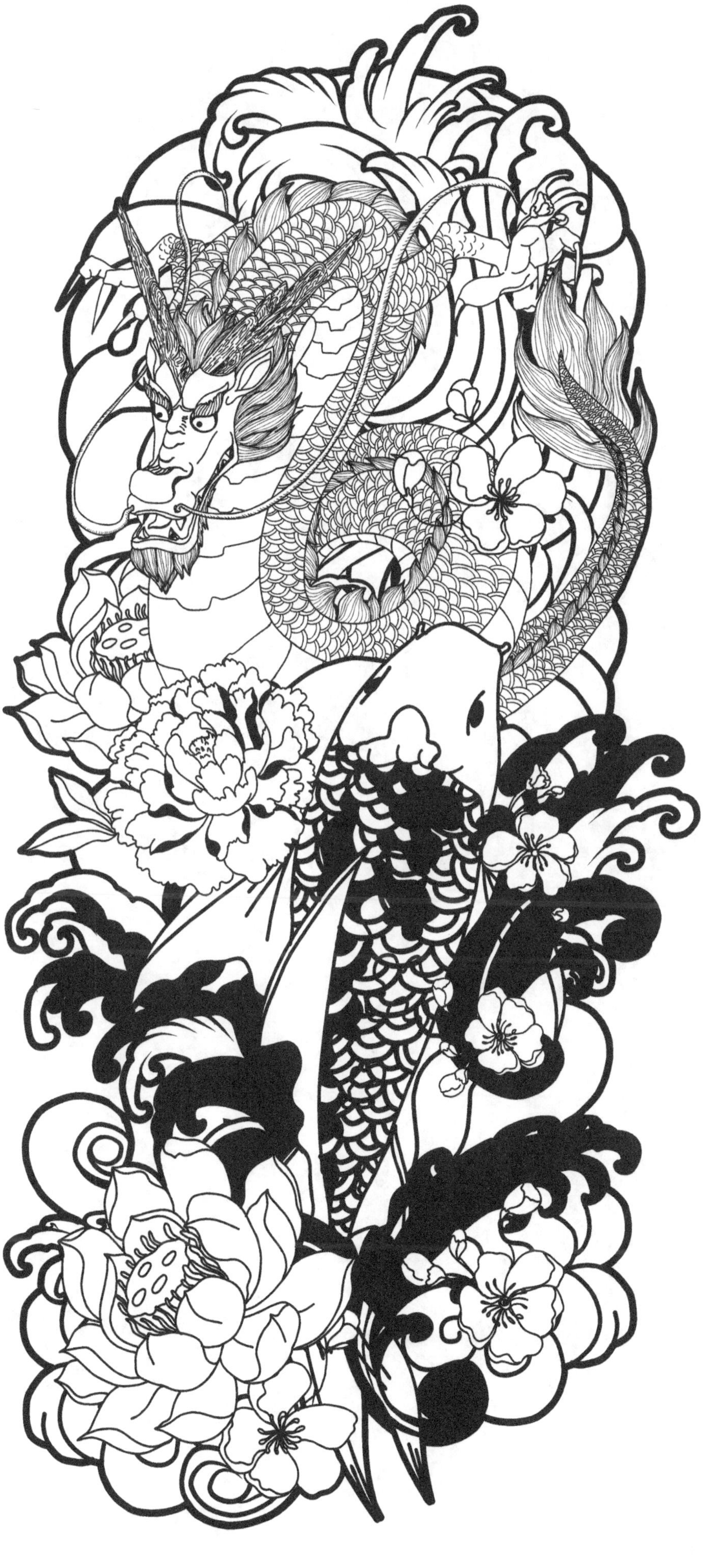

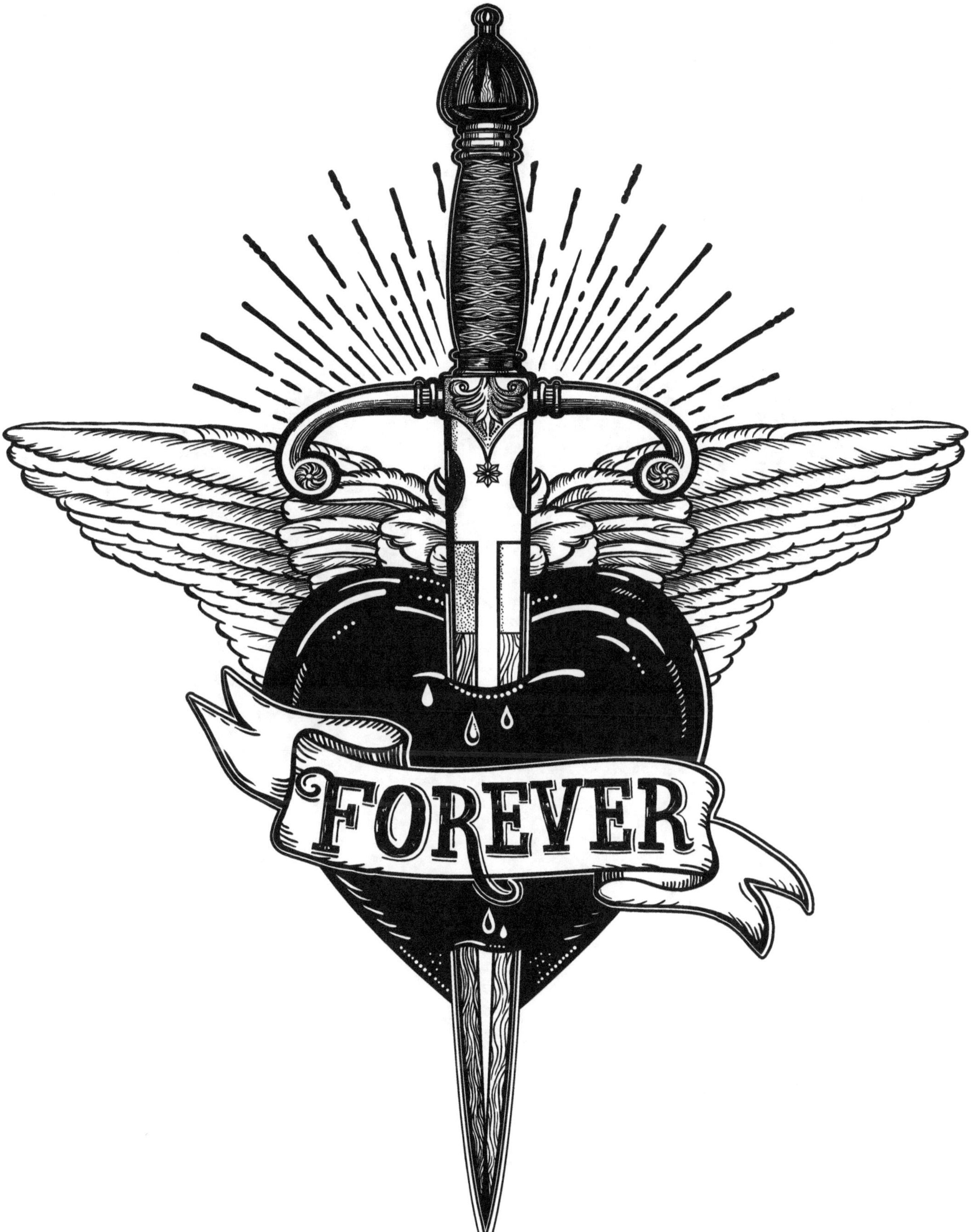
FOREVER

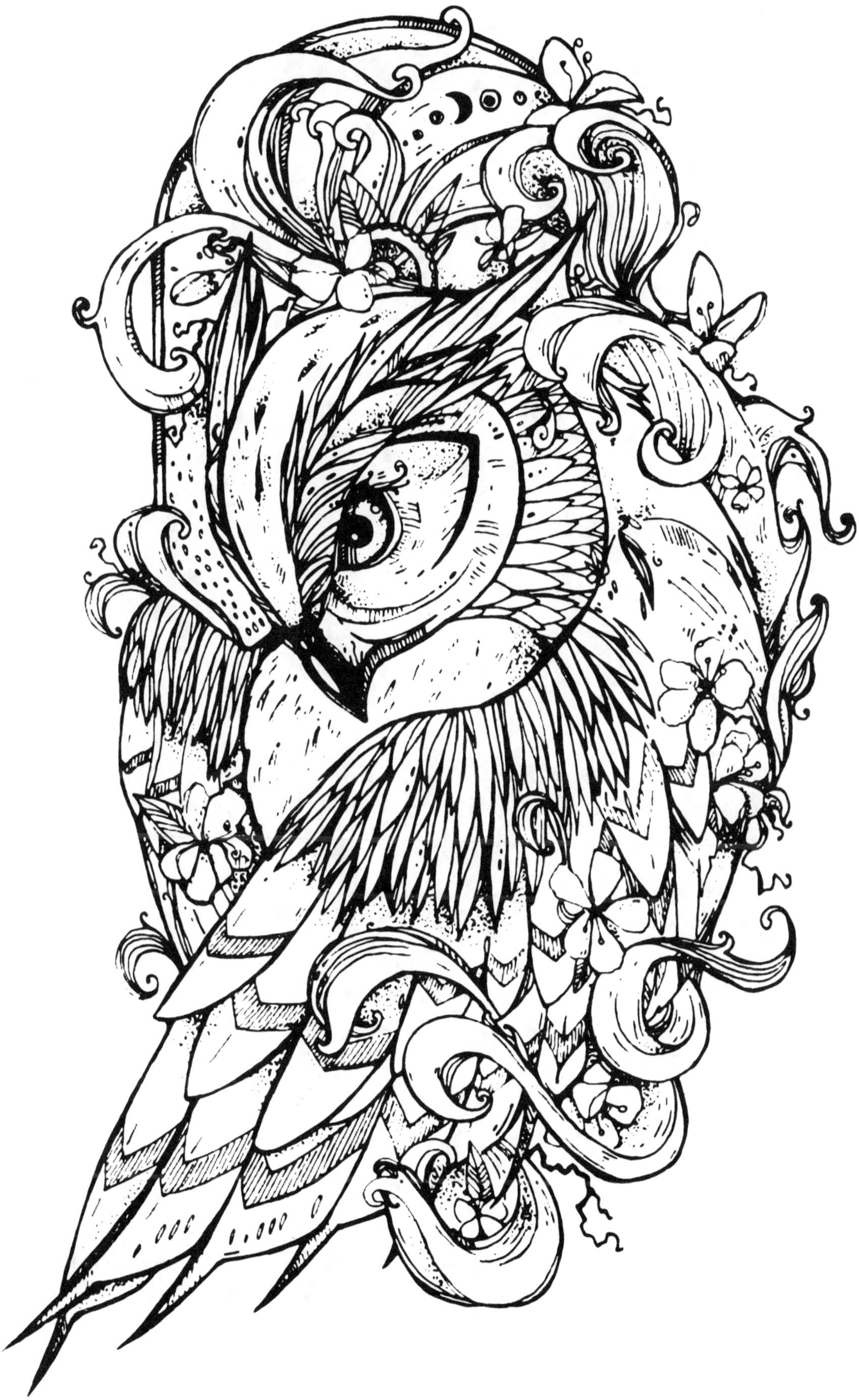

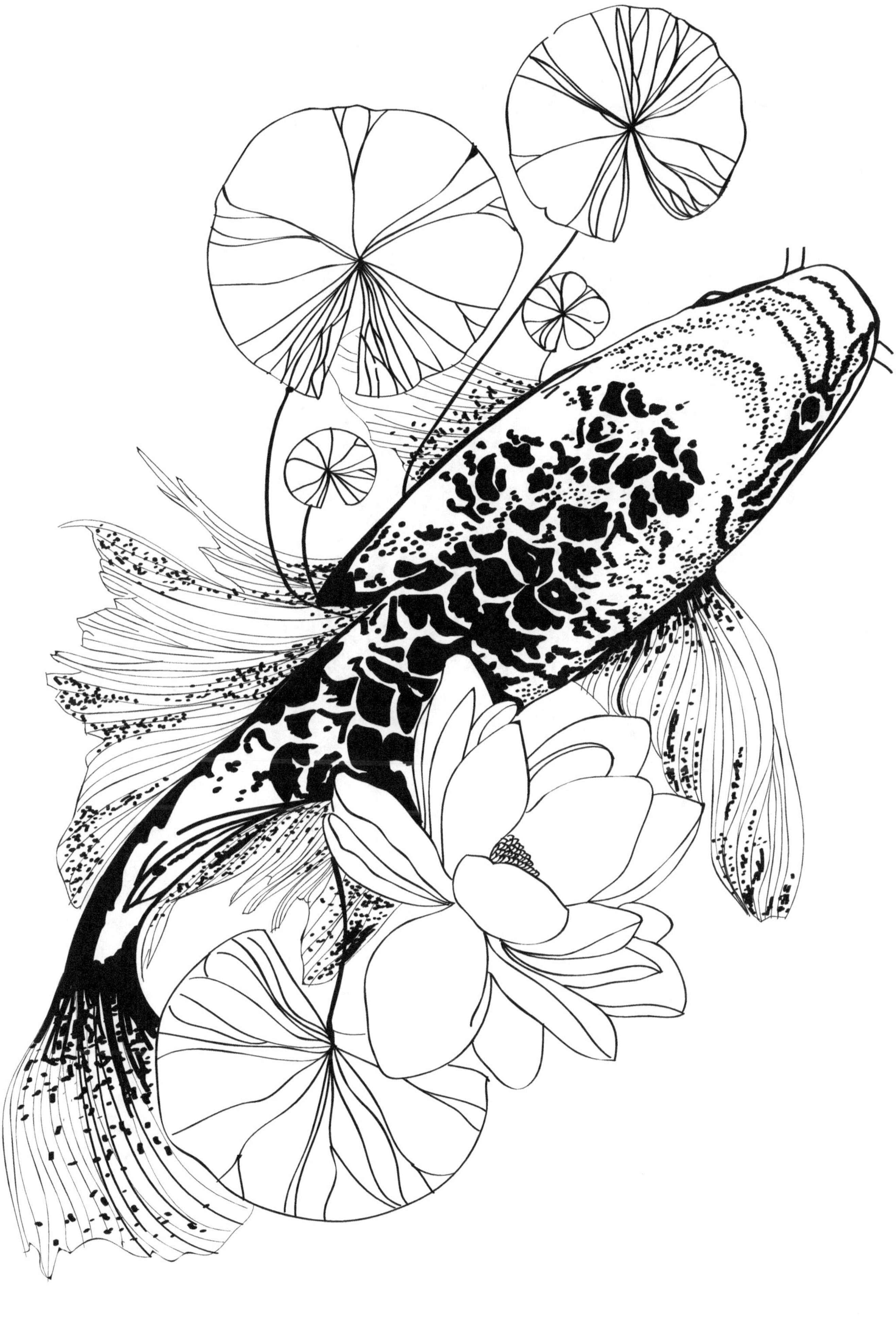

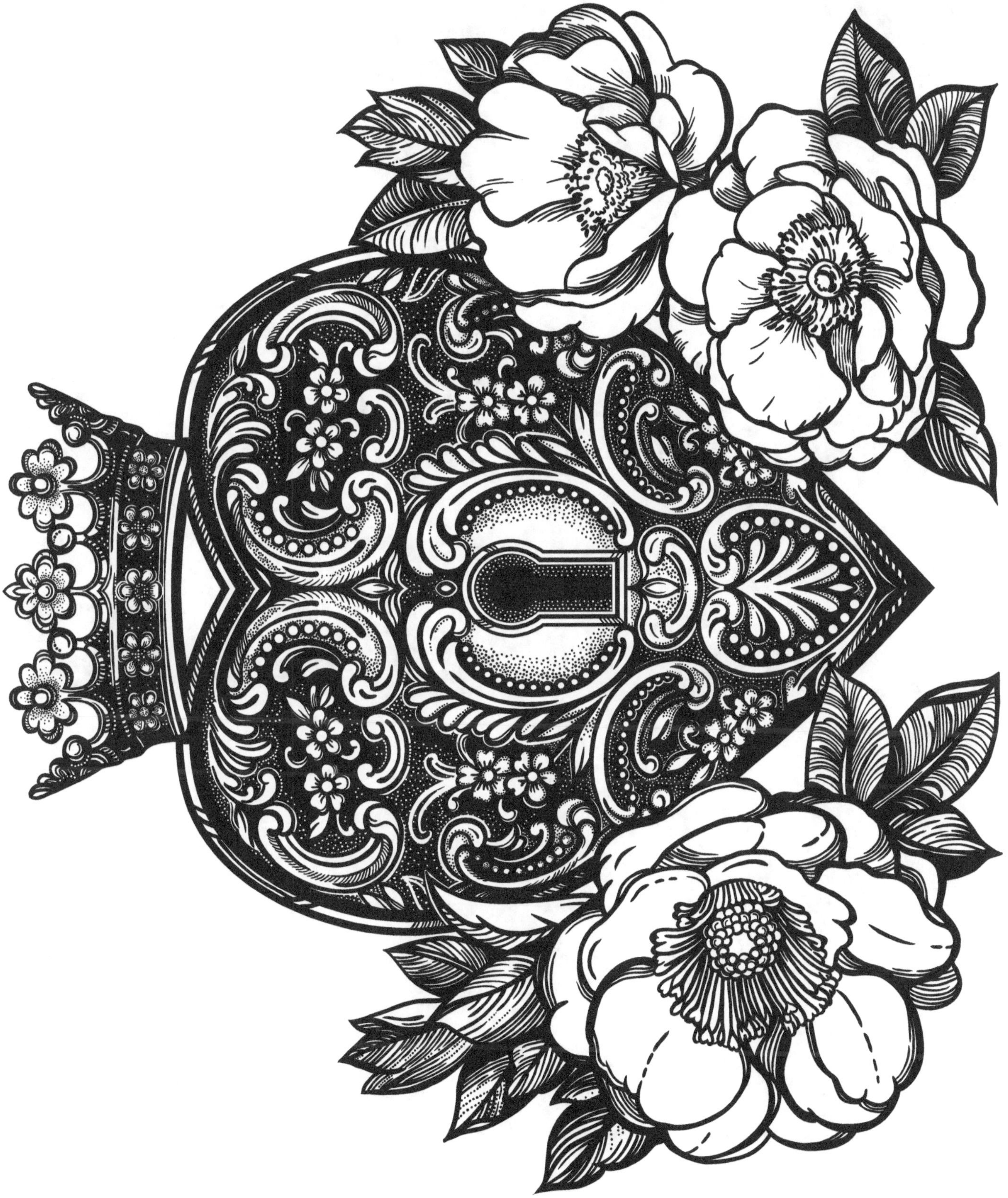

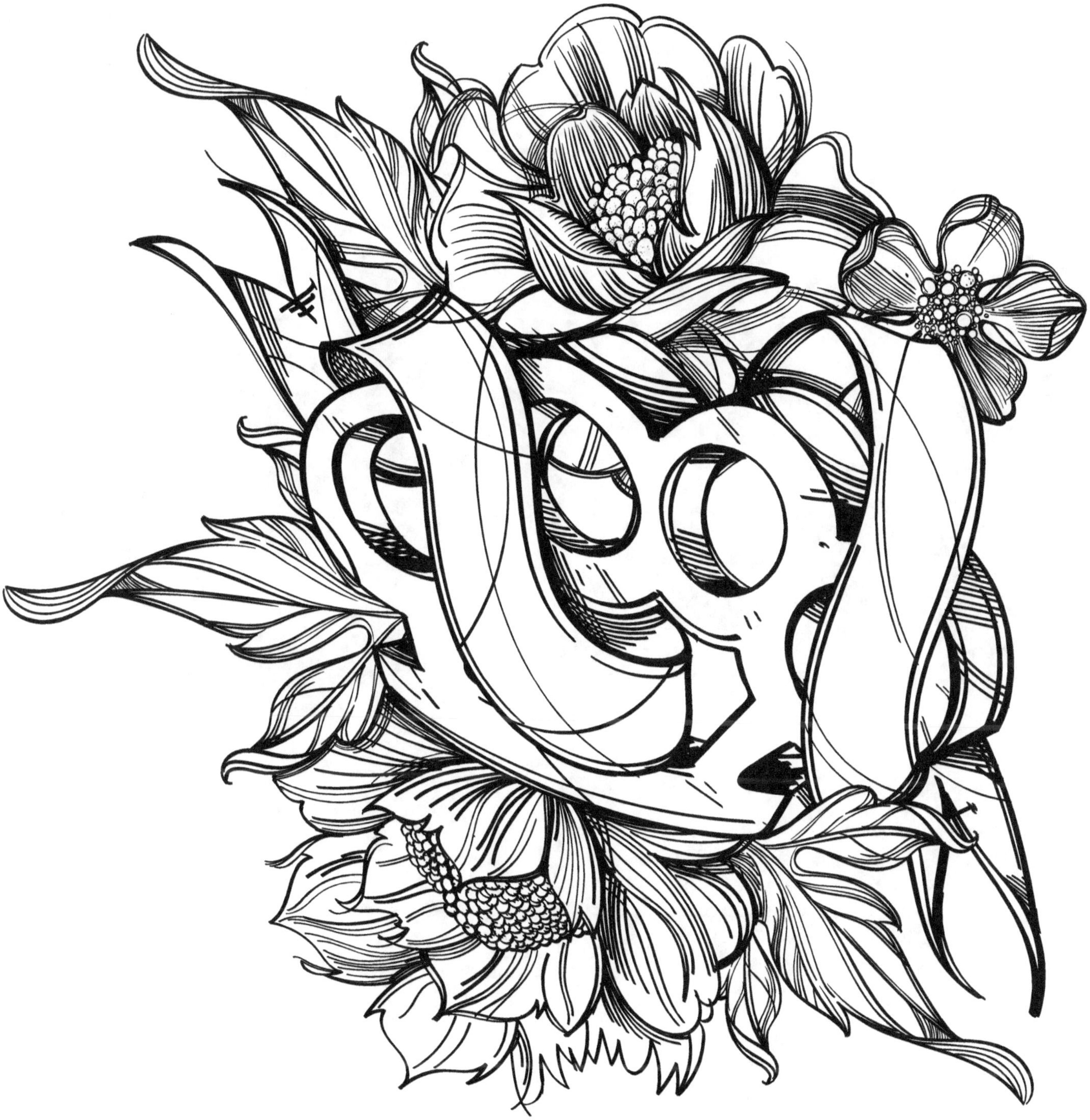

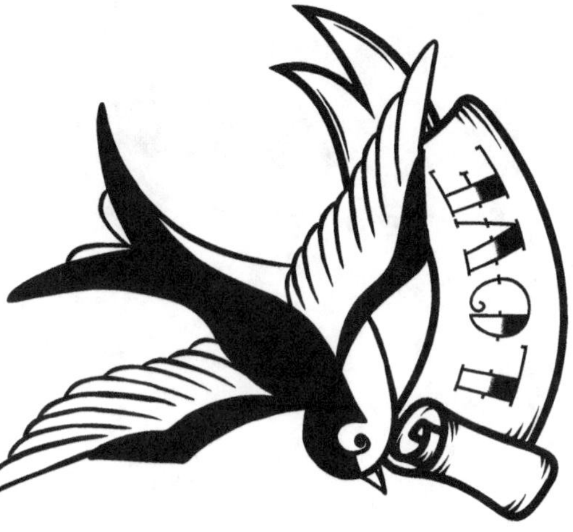
LOVE

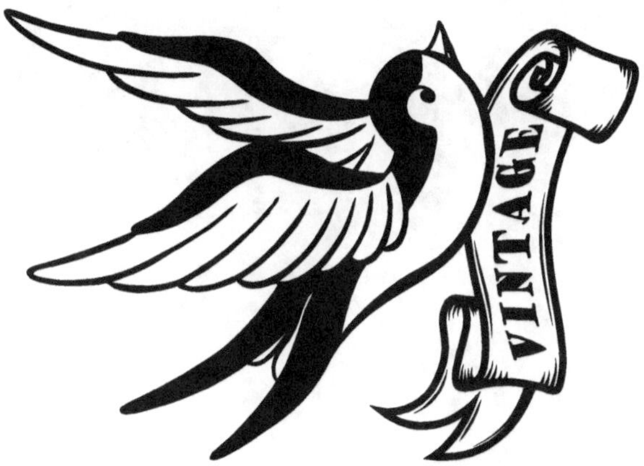
VINTAGE

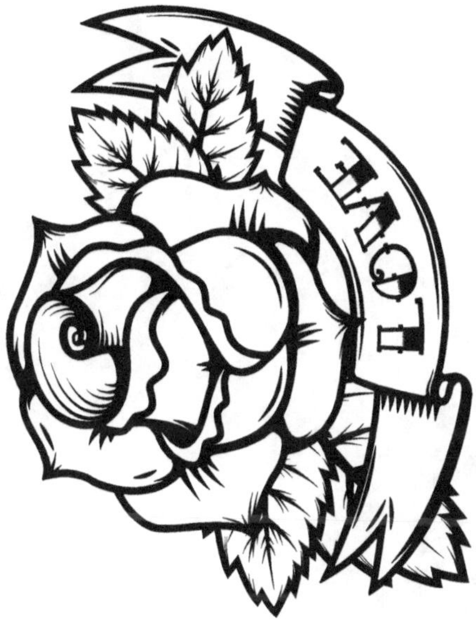
LOVE

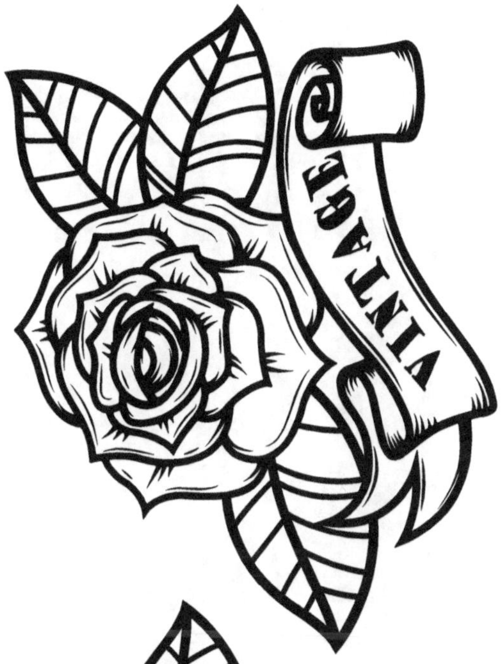
VINTAGE

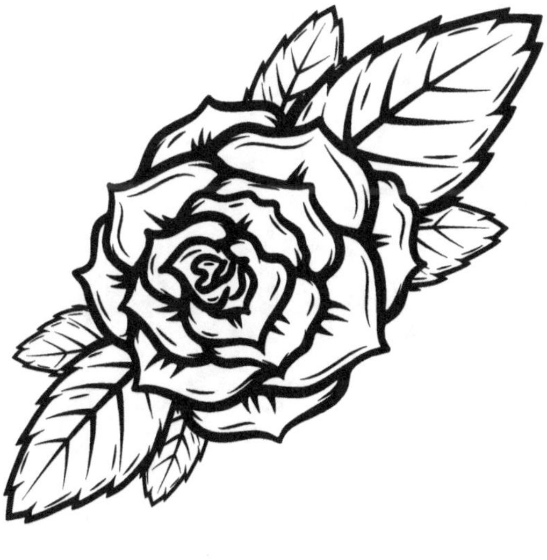

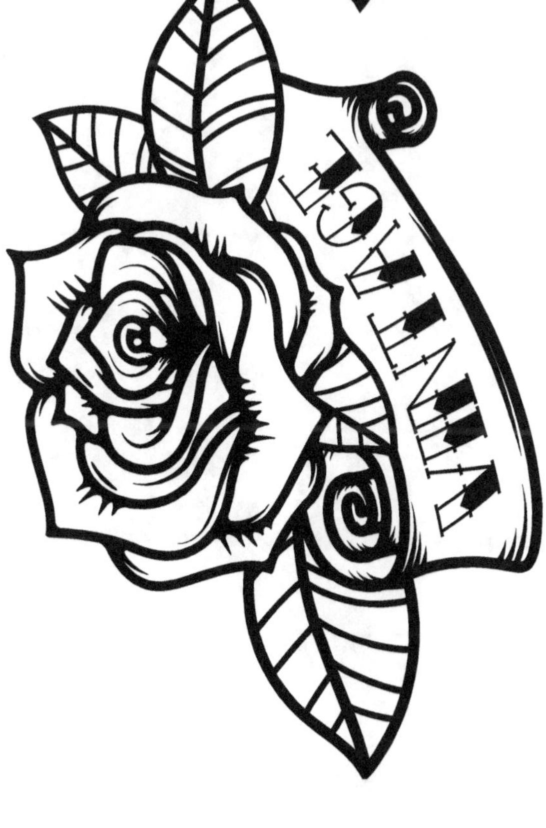
VINTAGE

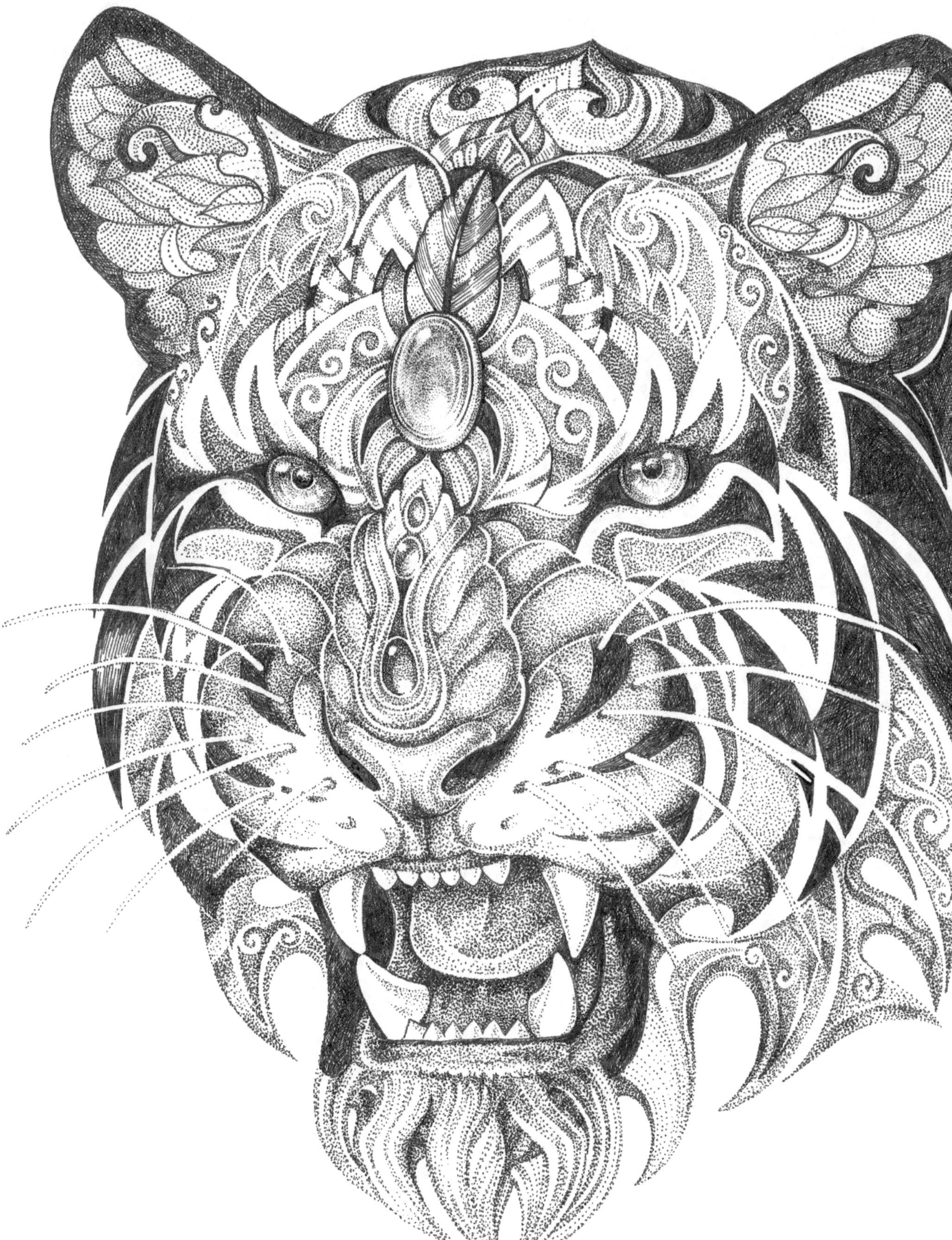

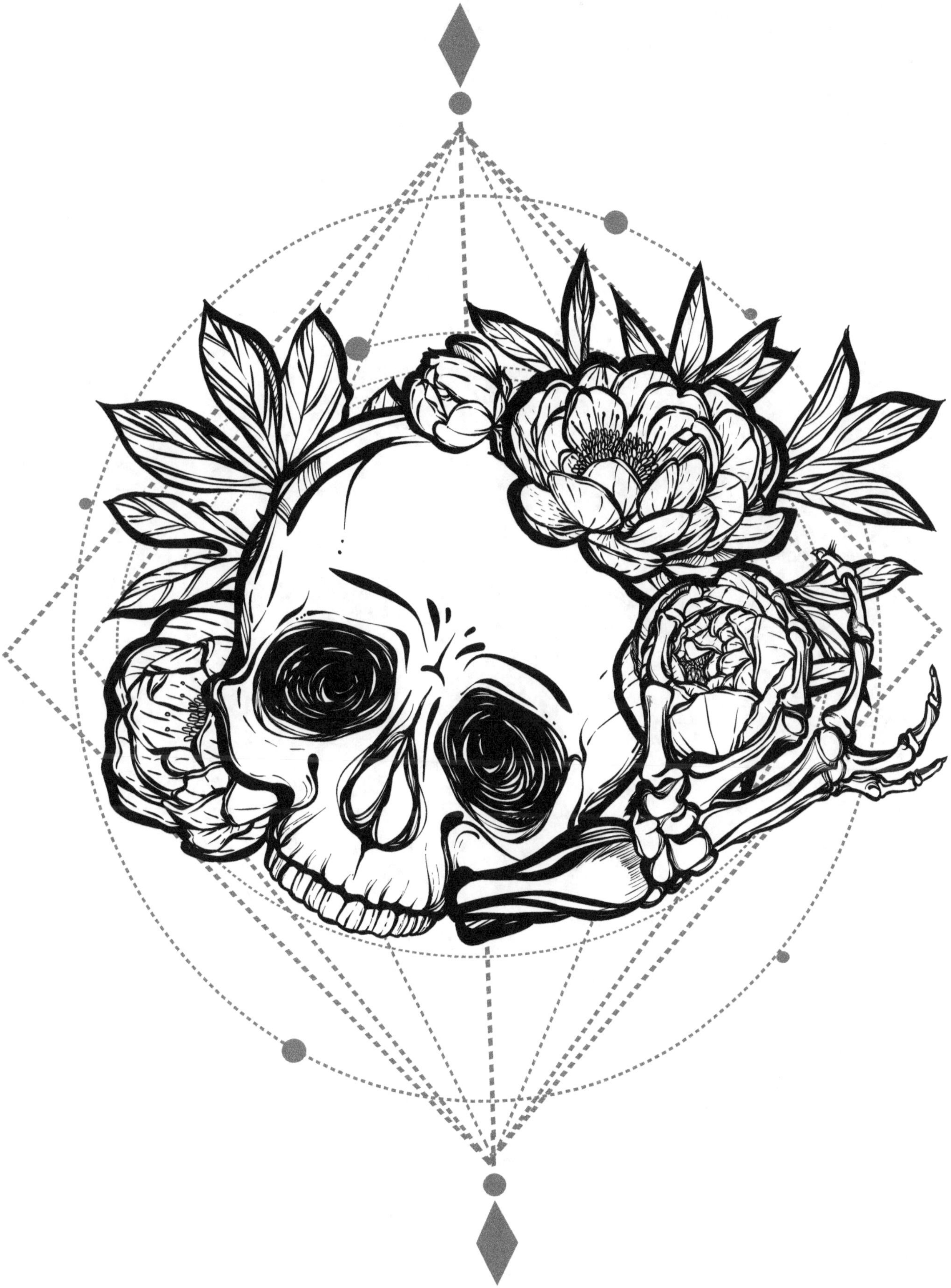

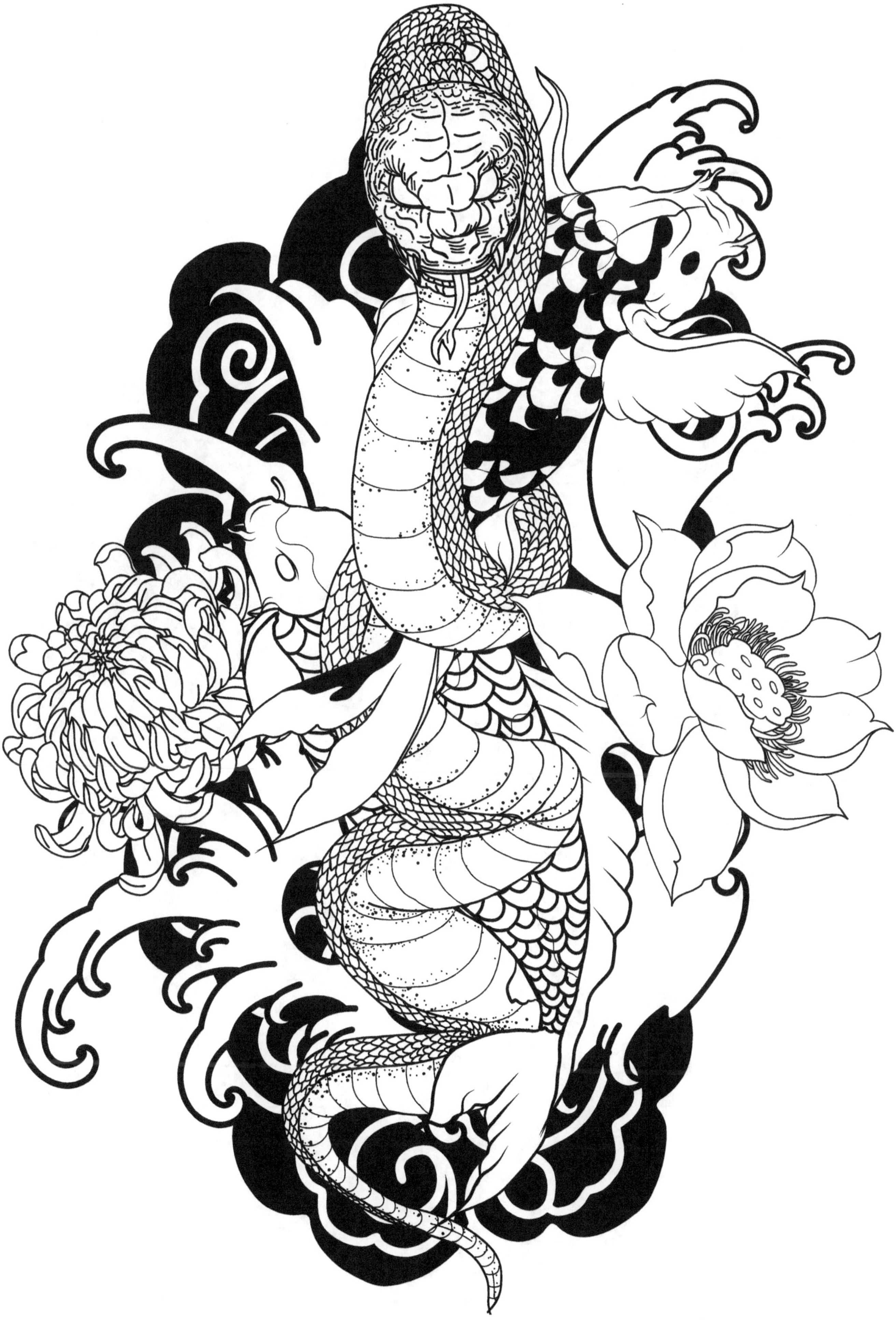

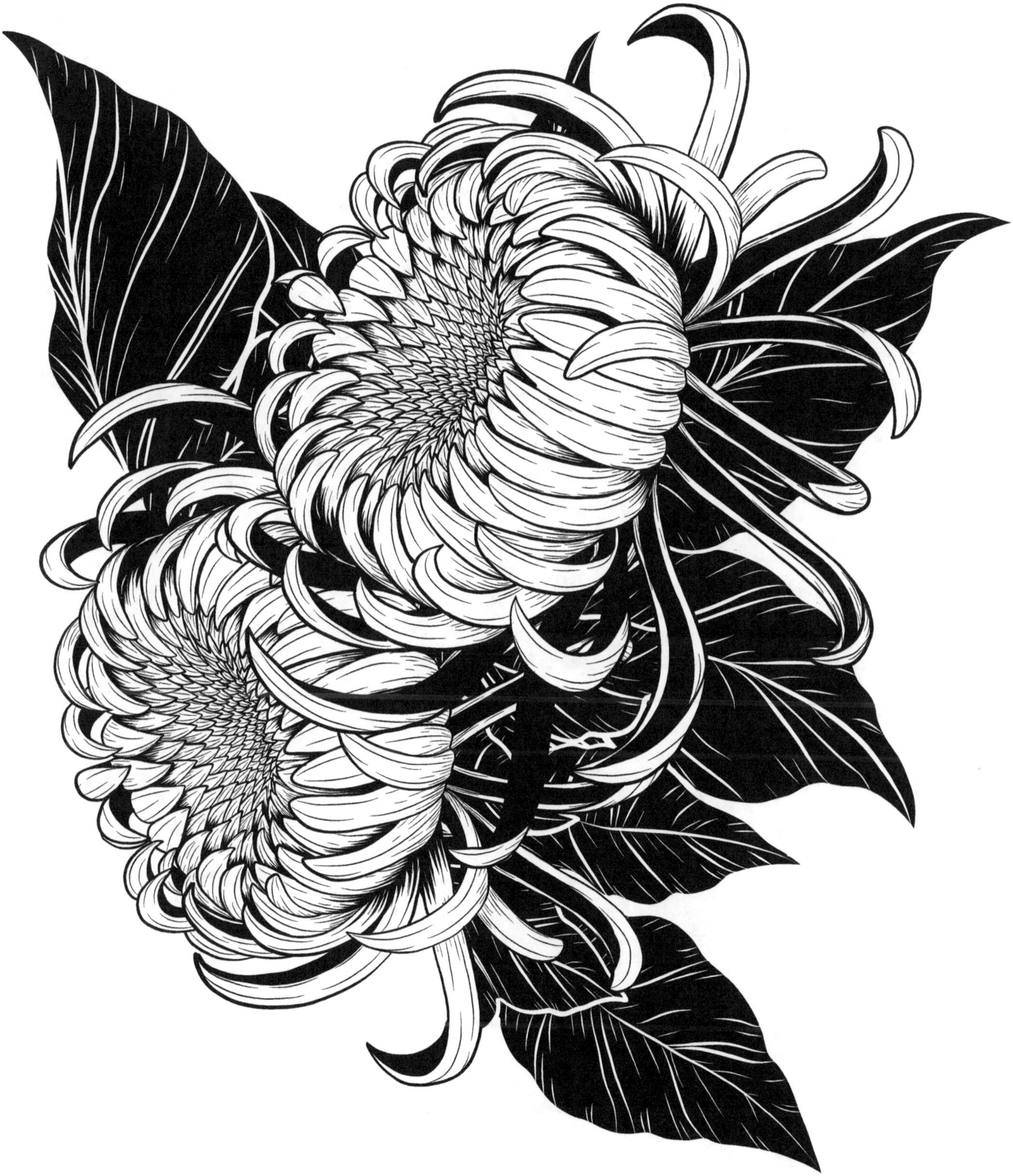

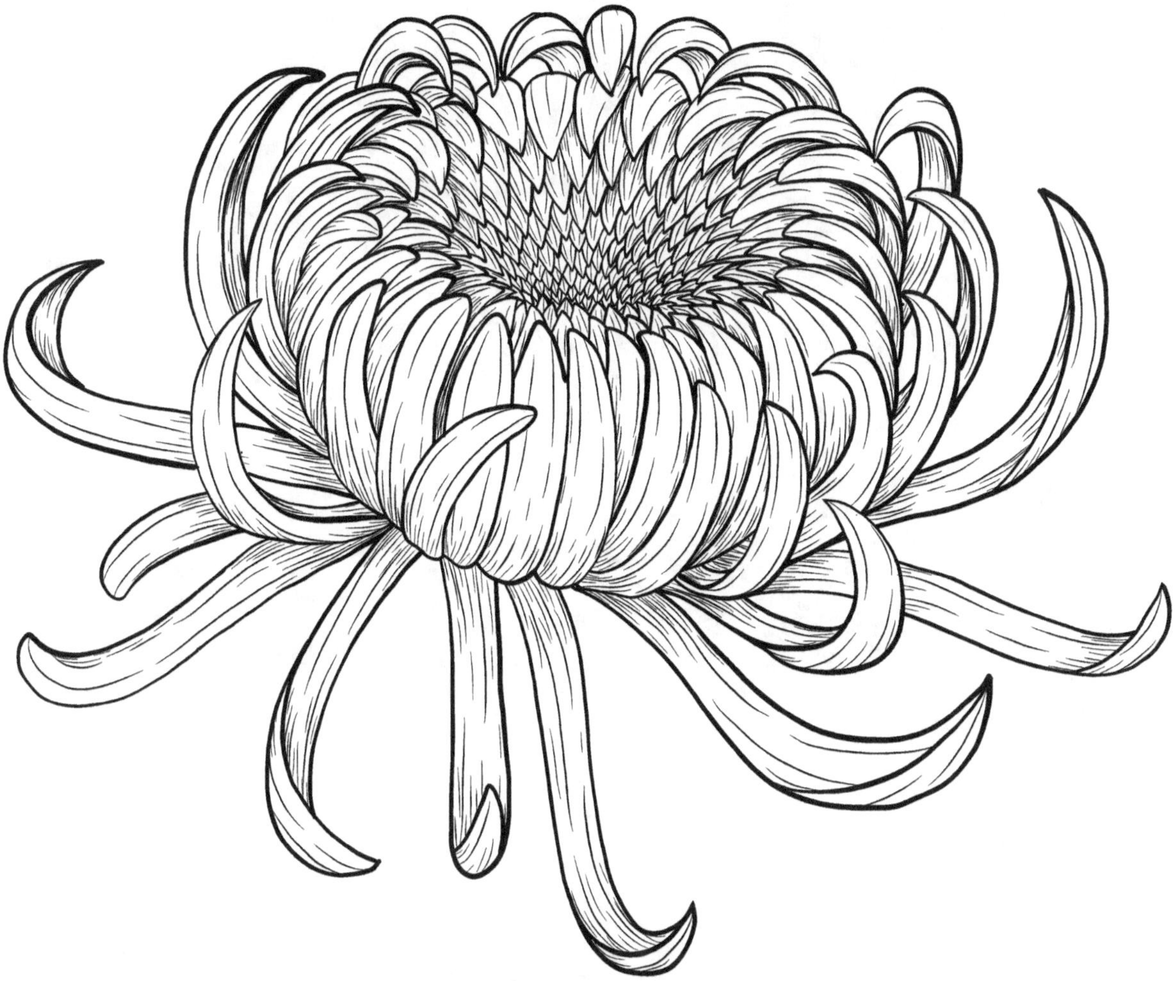

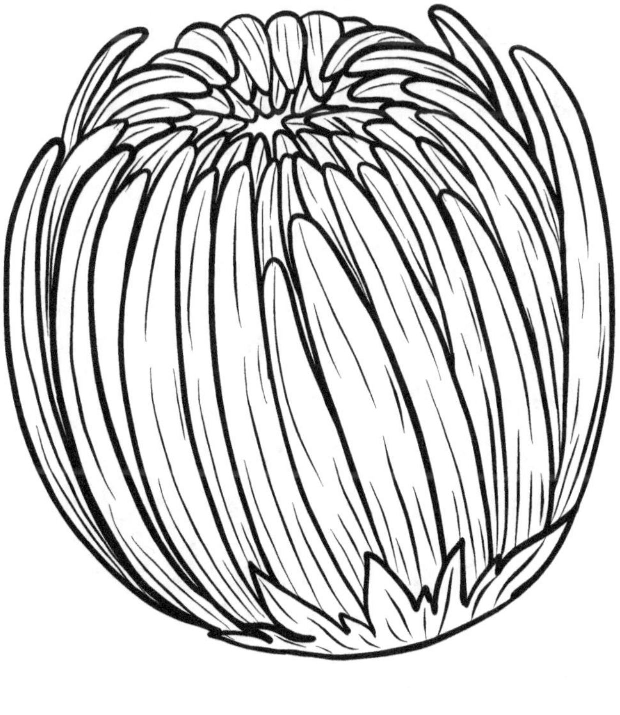

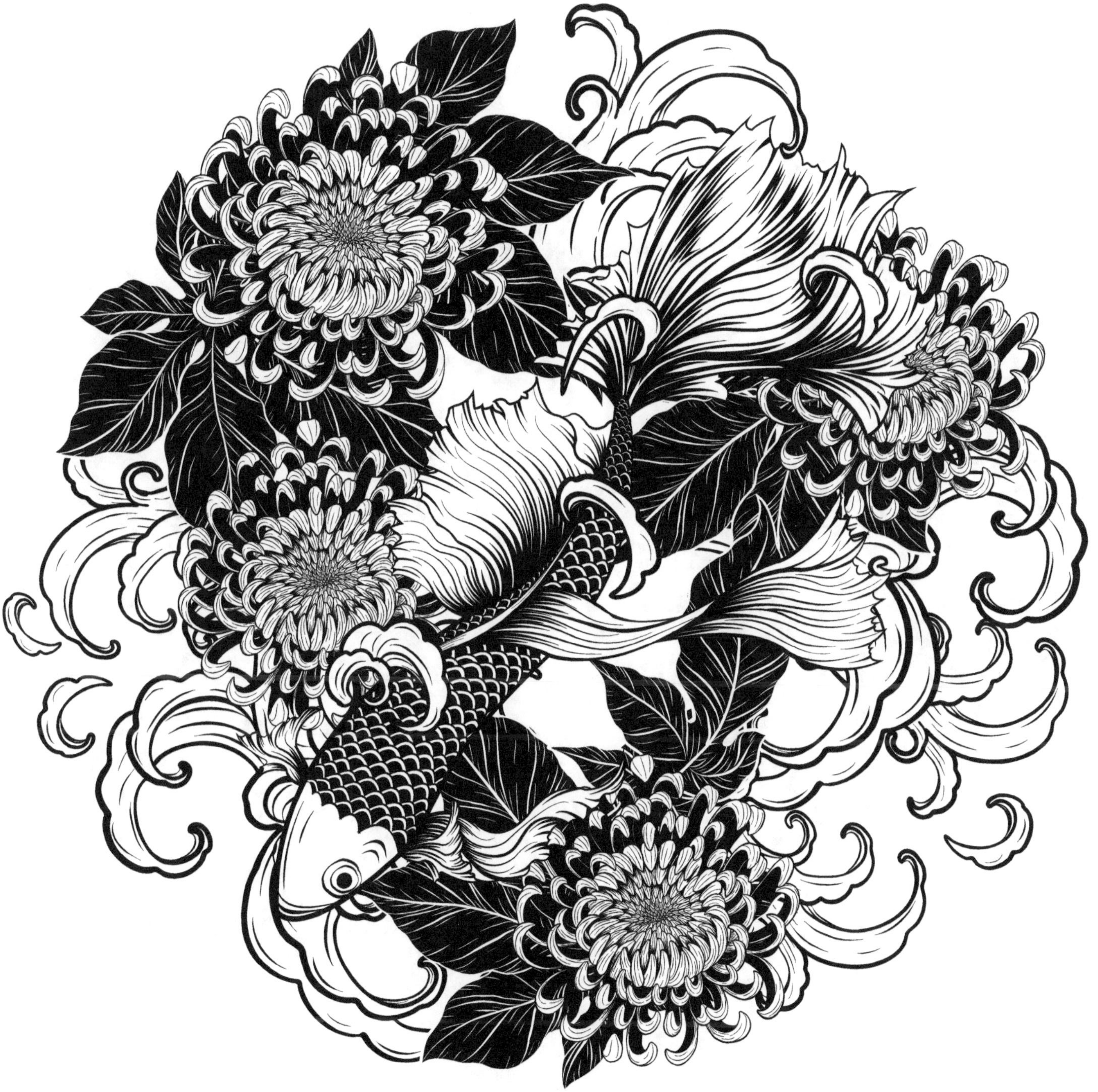

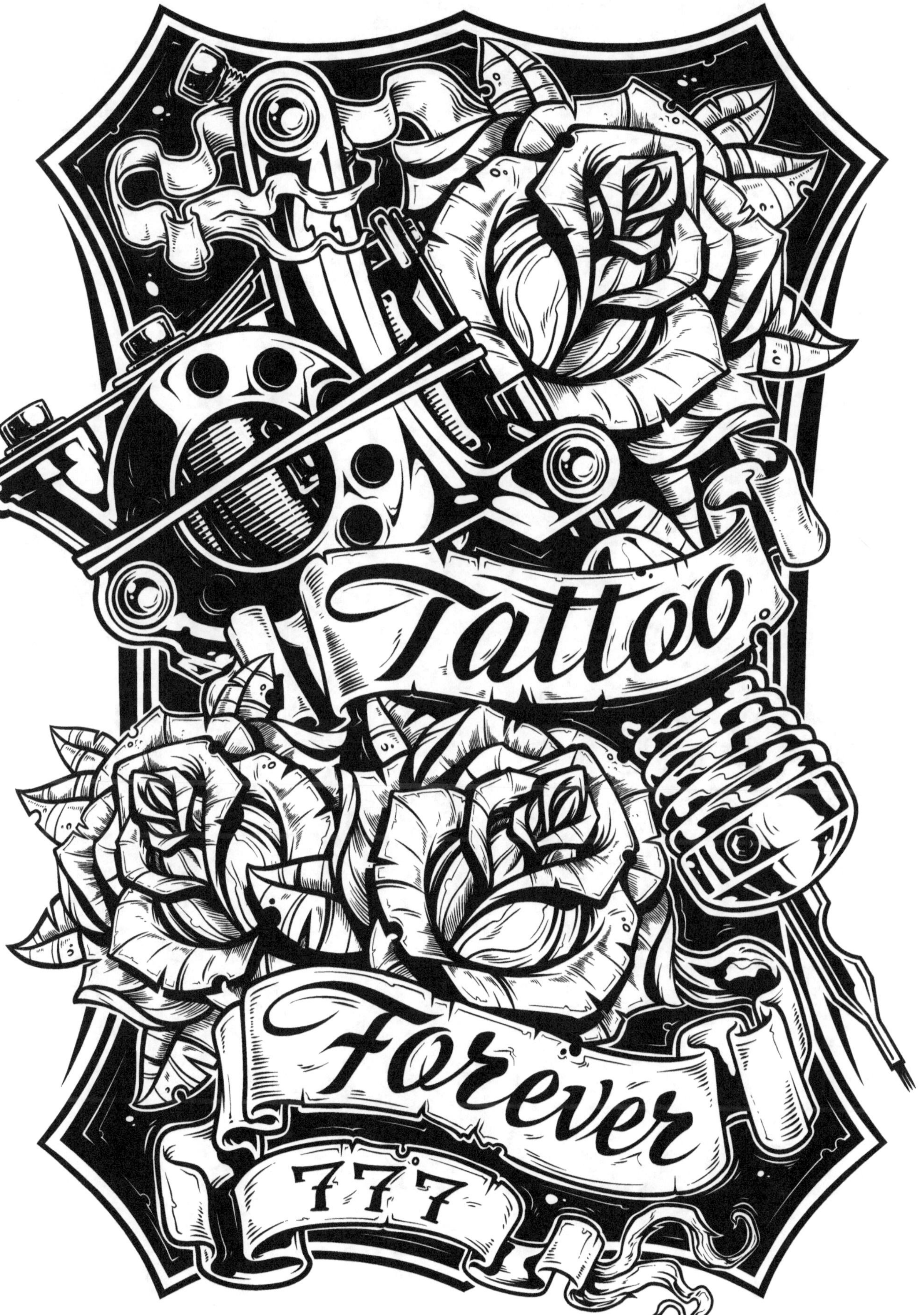
Tattoo
Forever
777

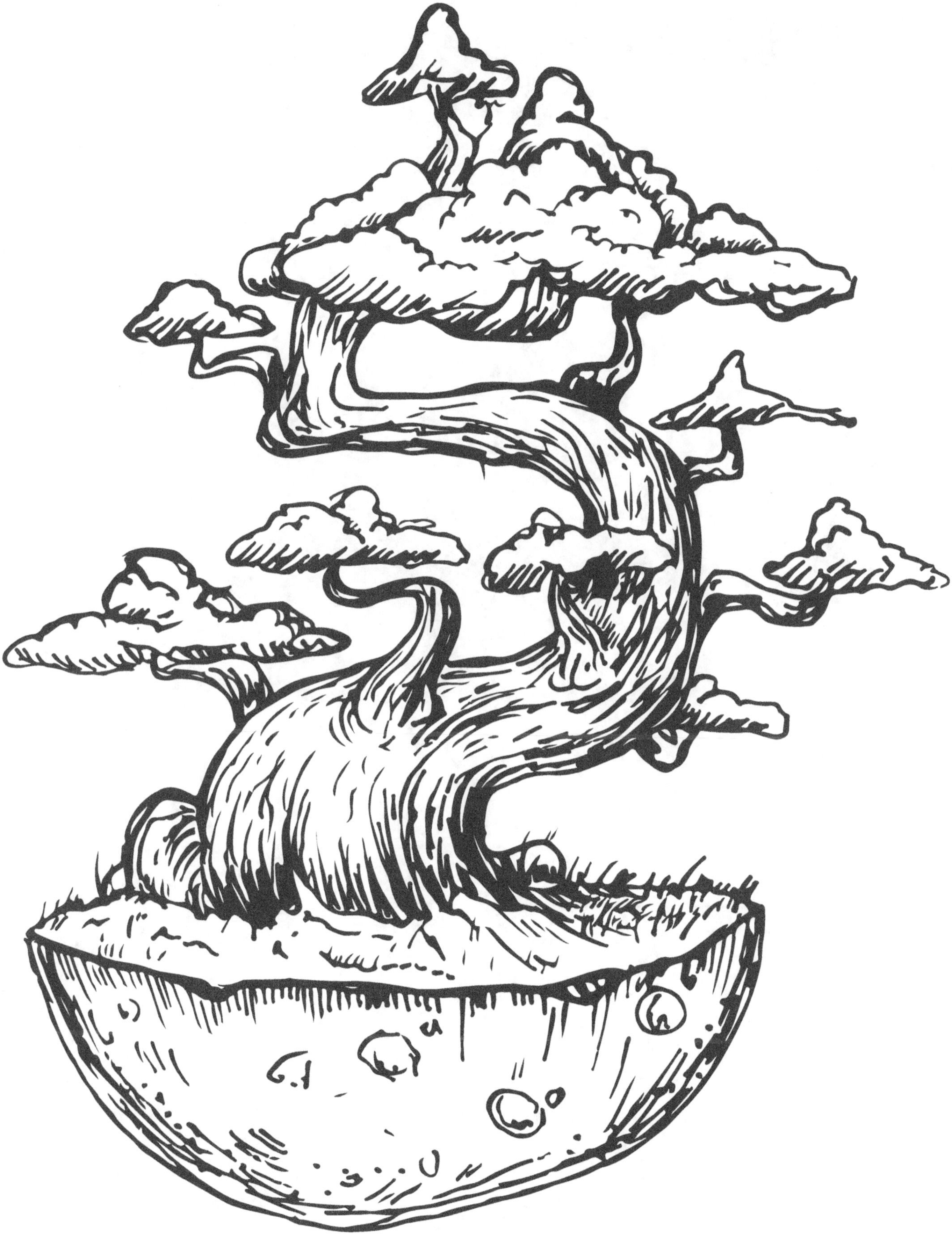

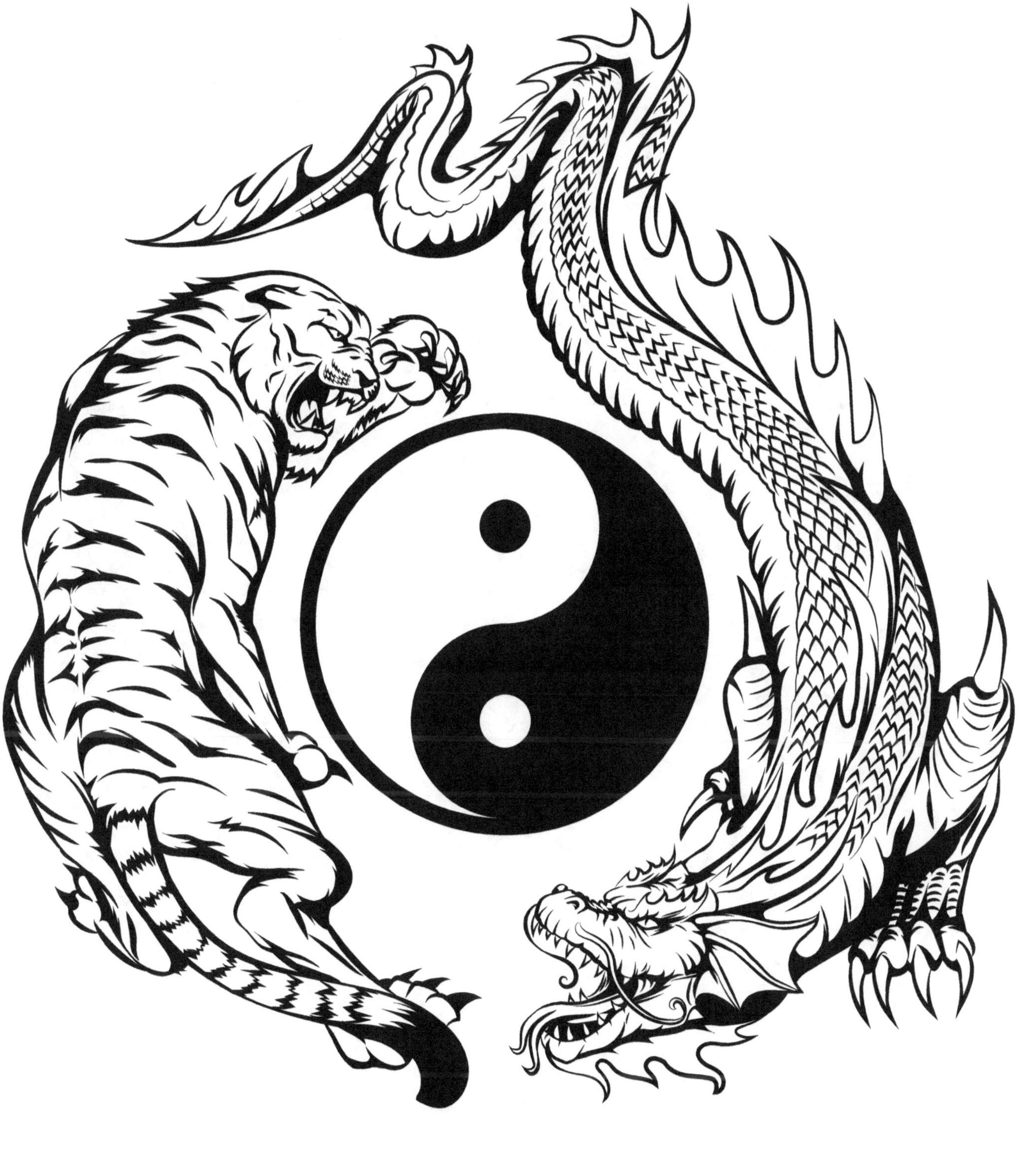

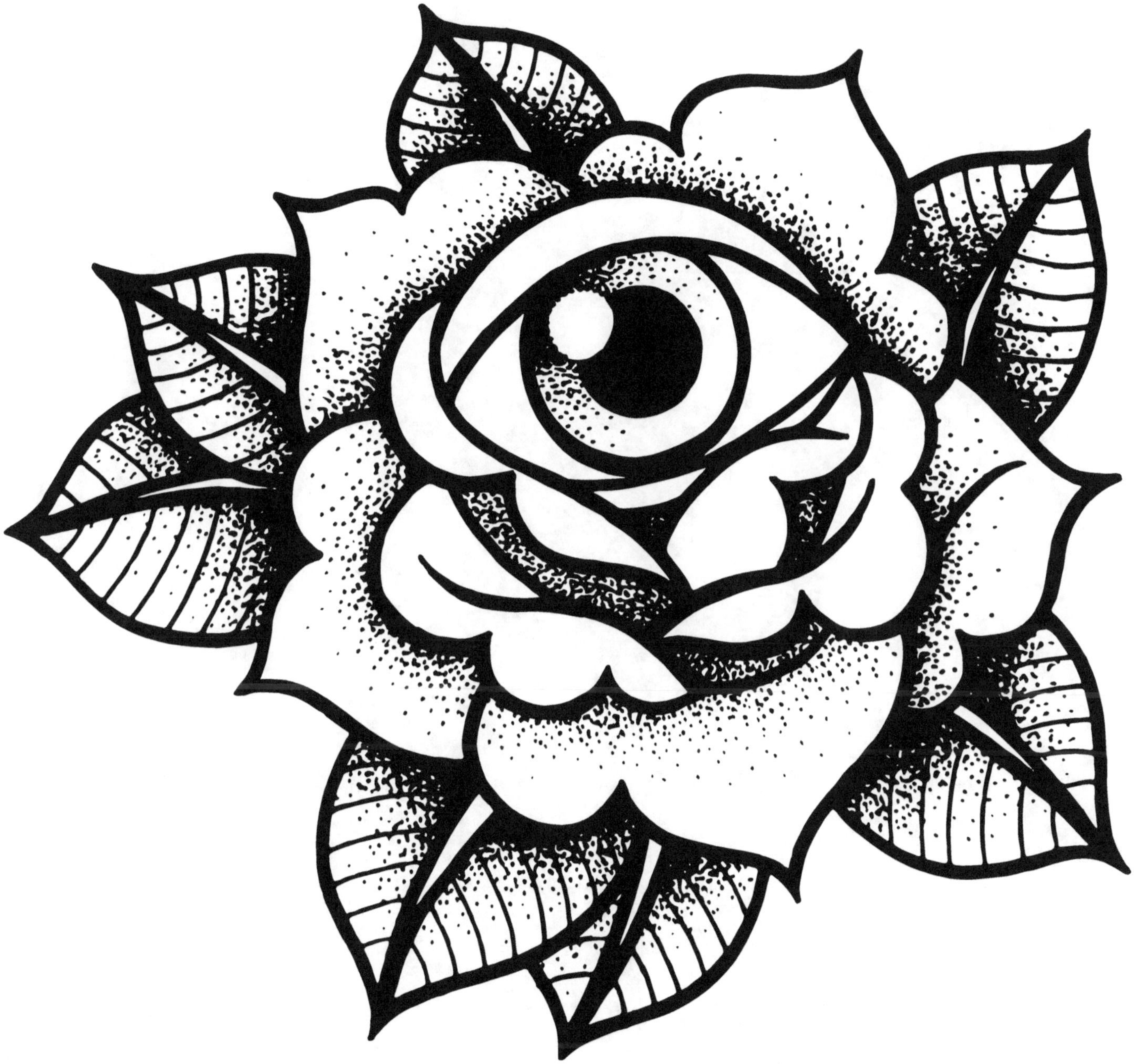

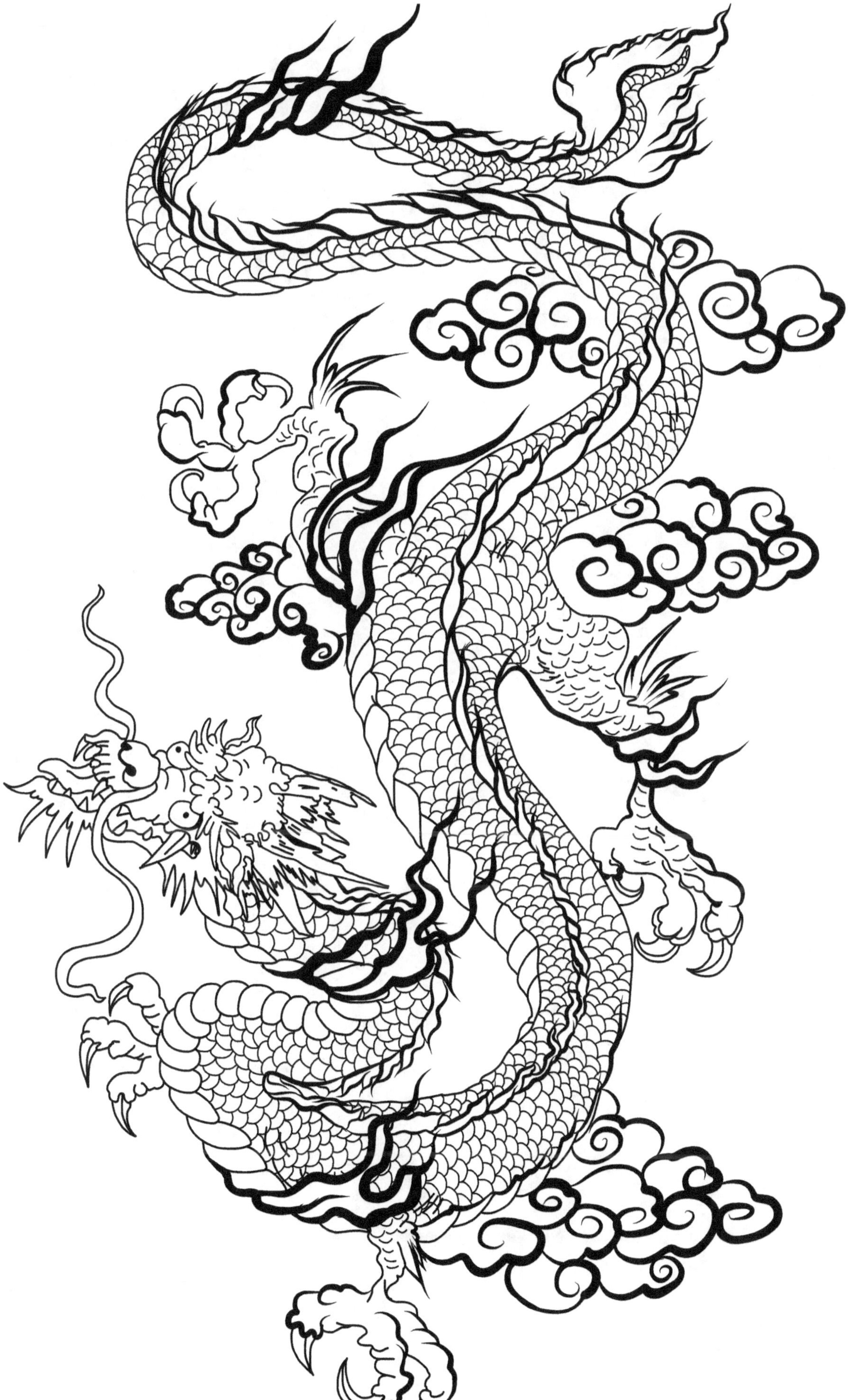

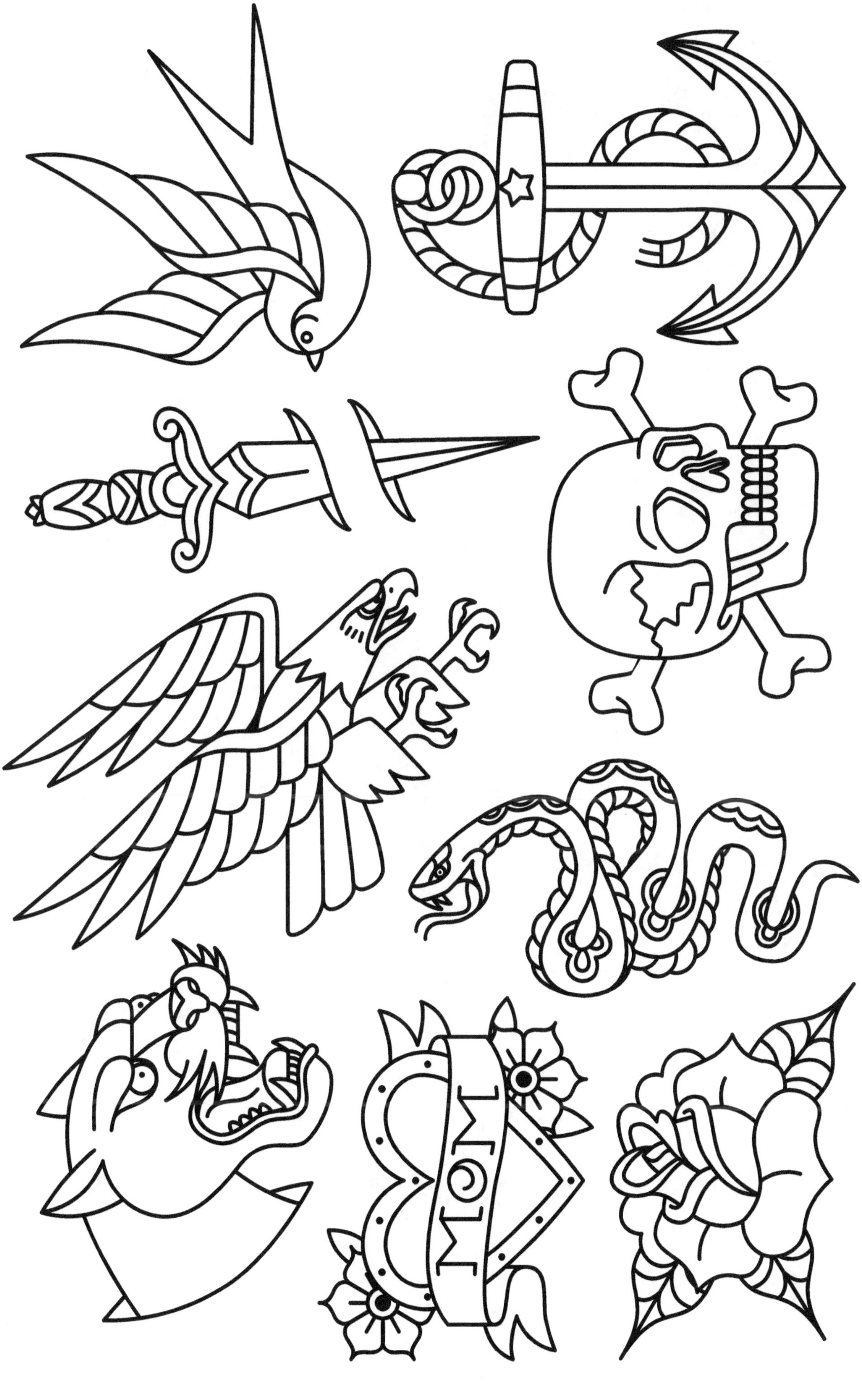
MOM

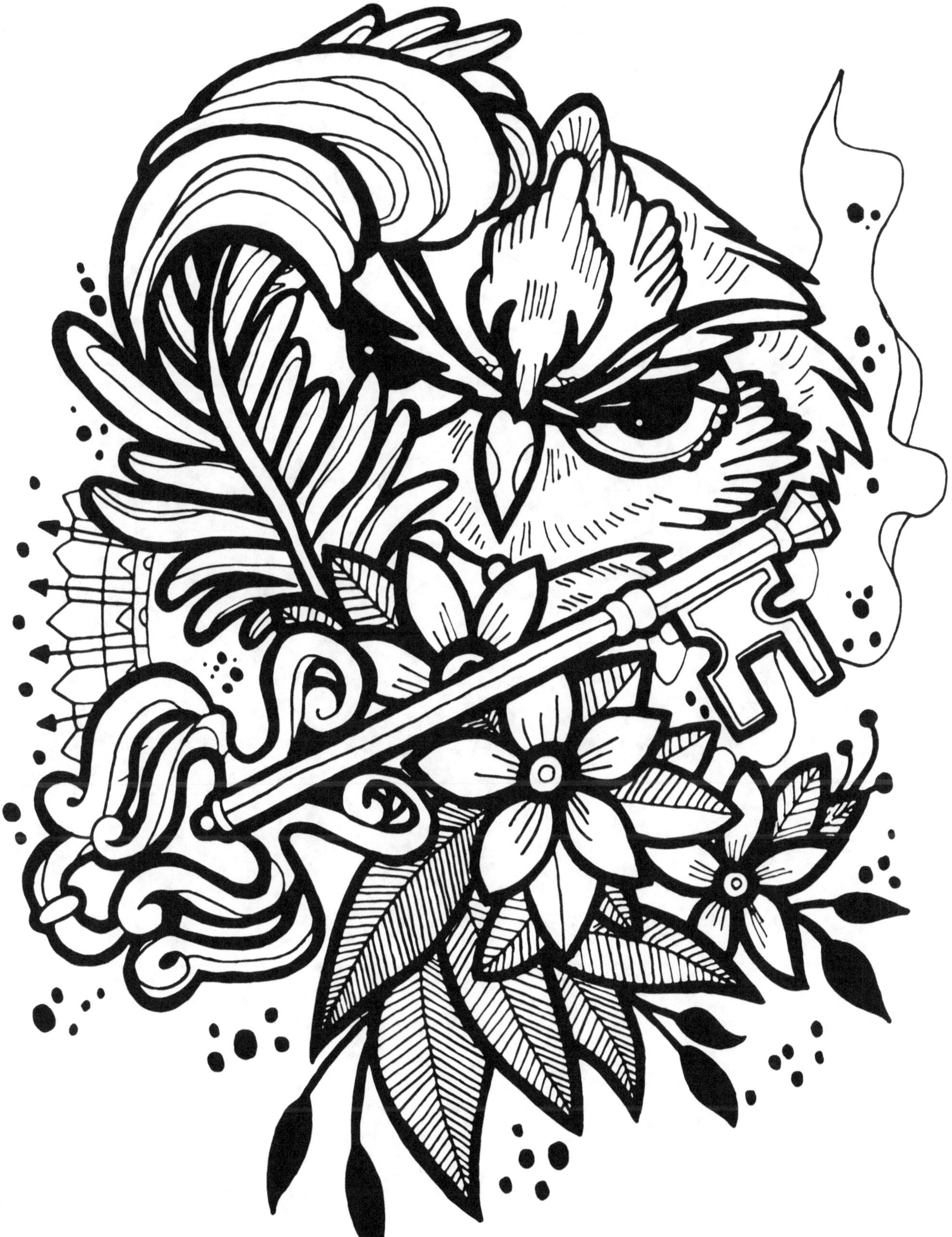

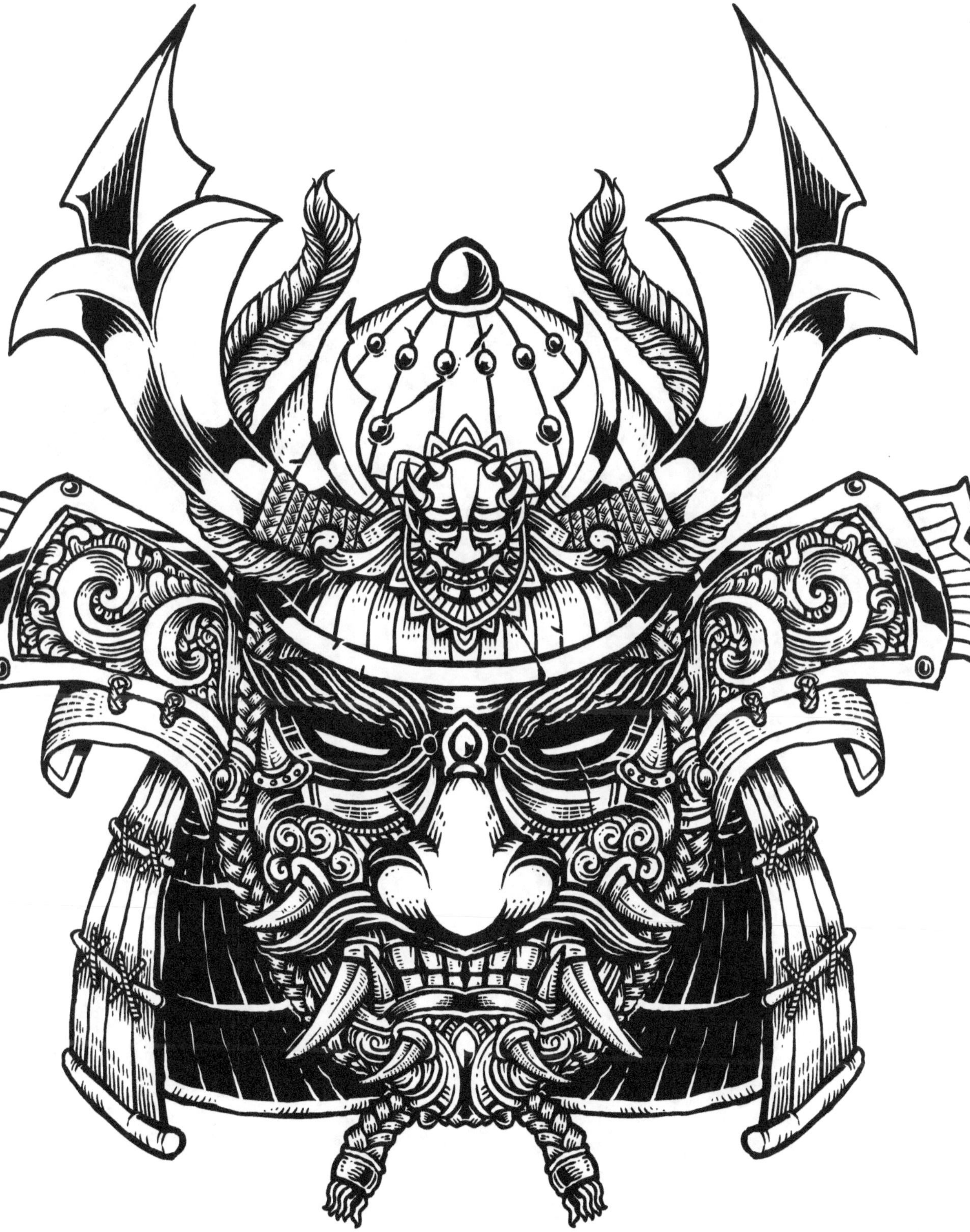

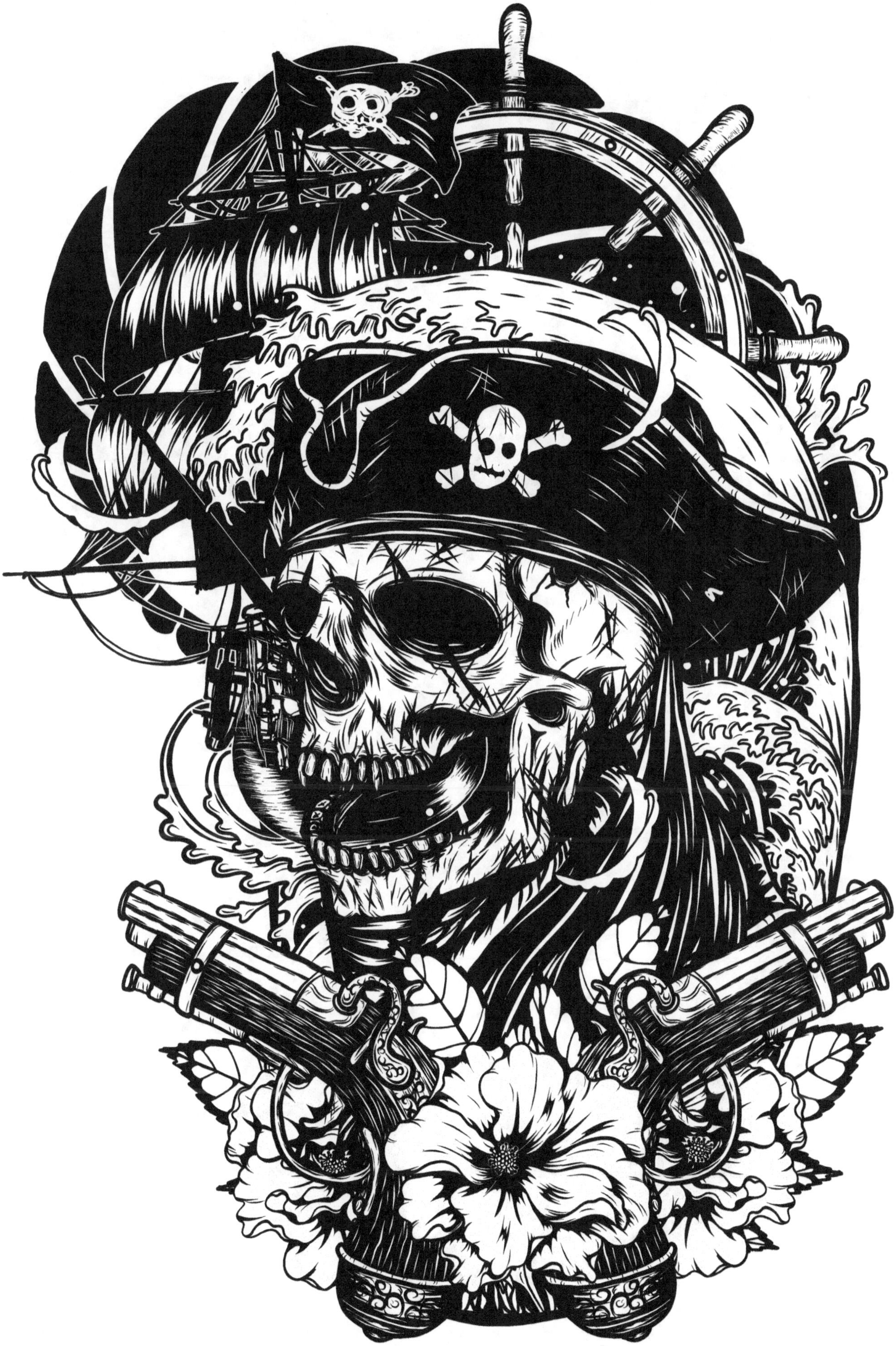

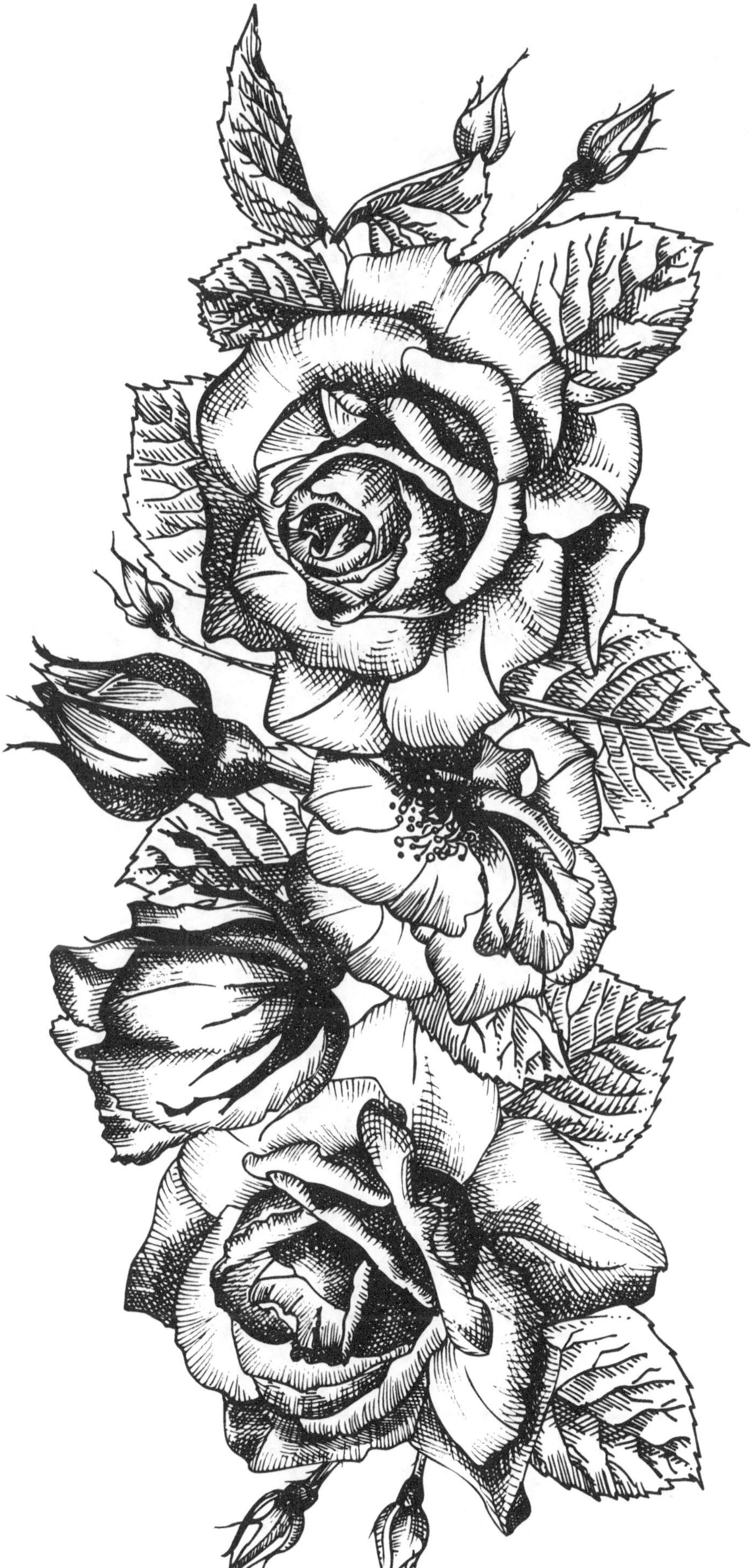

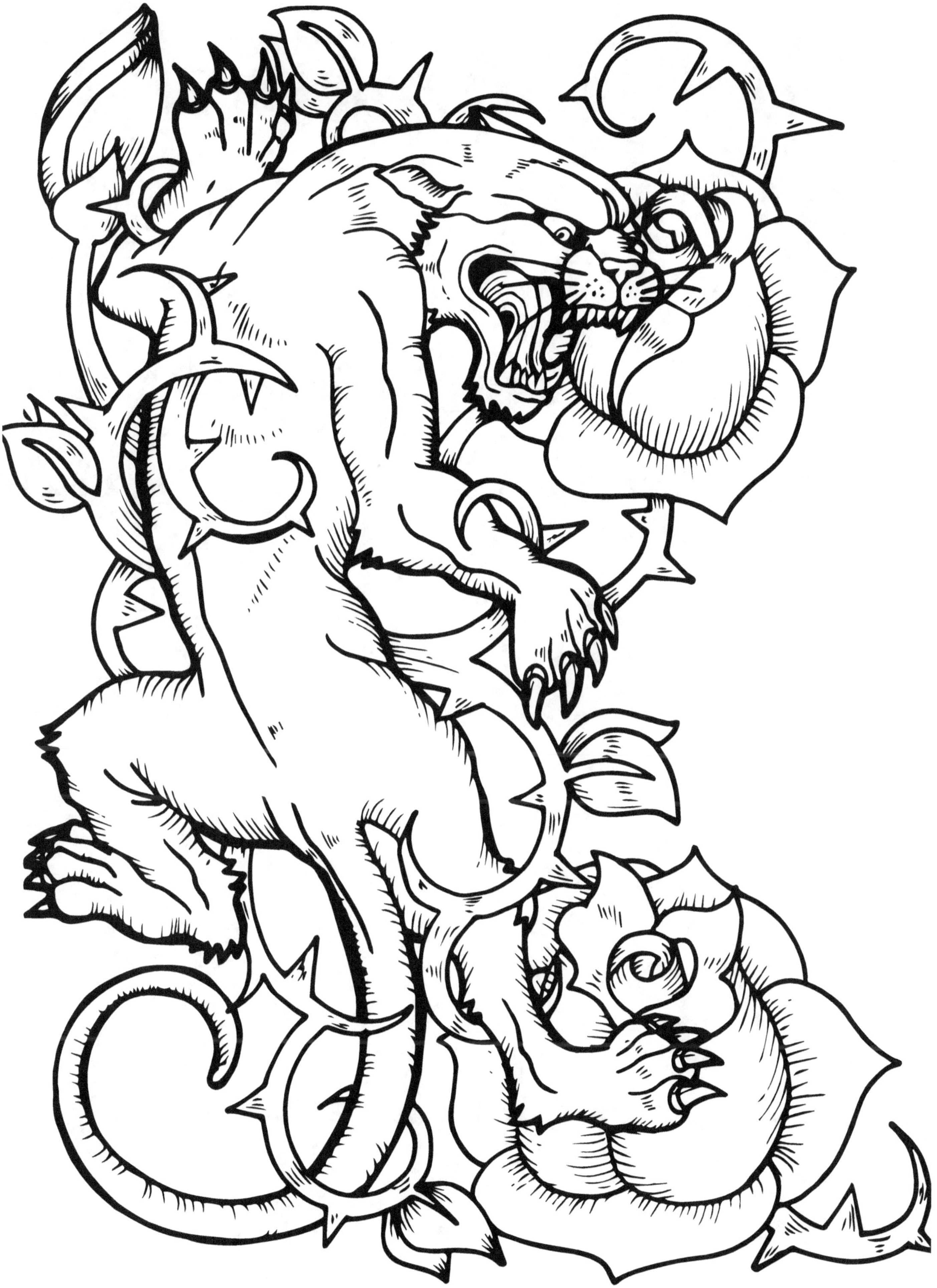

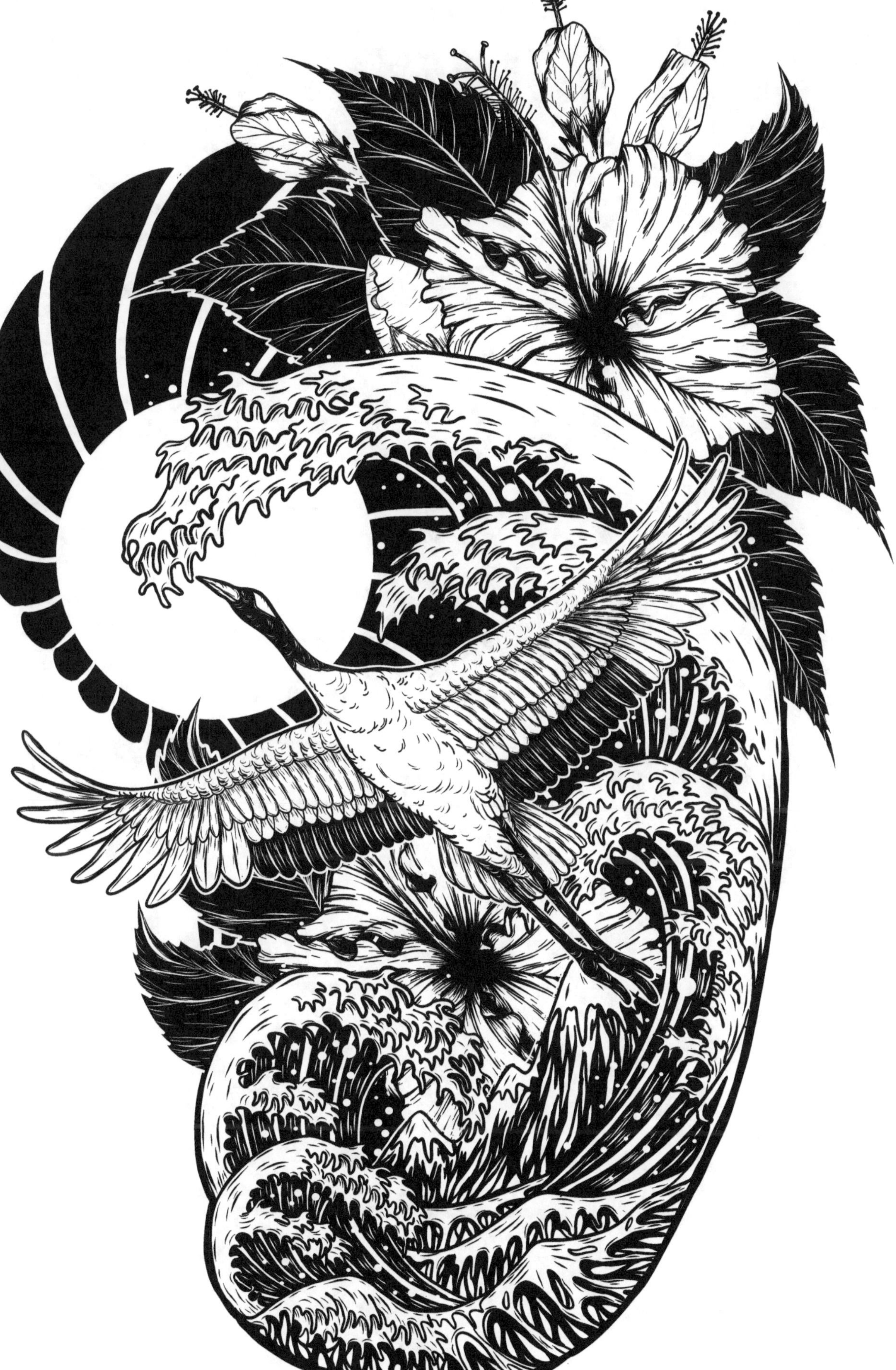

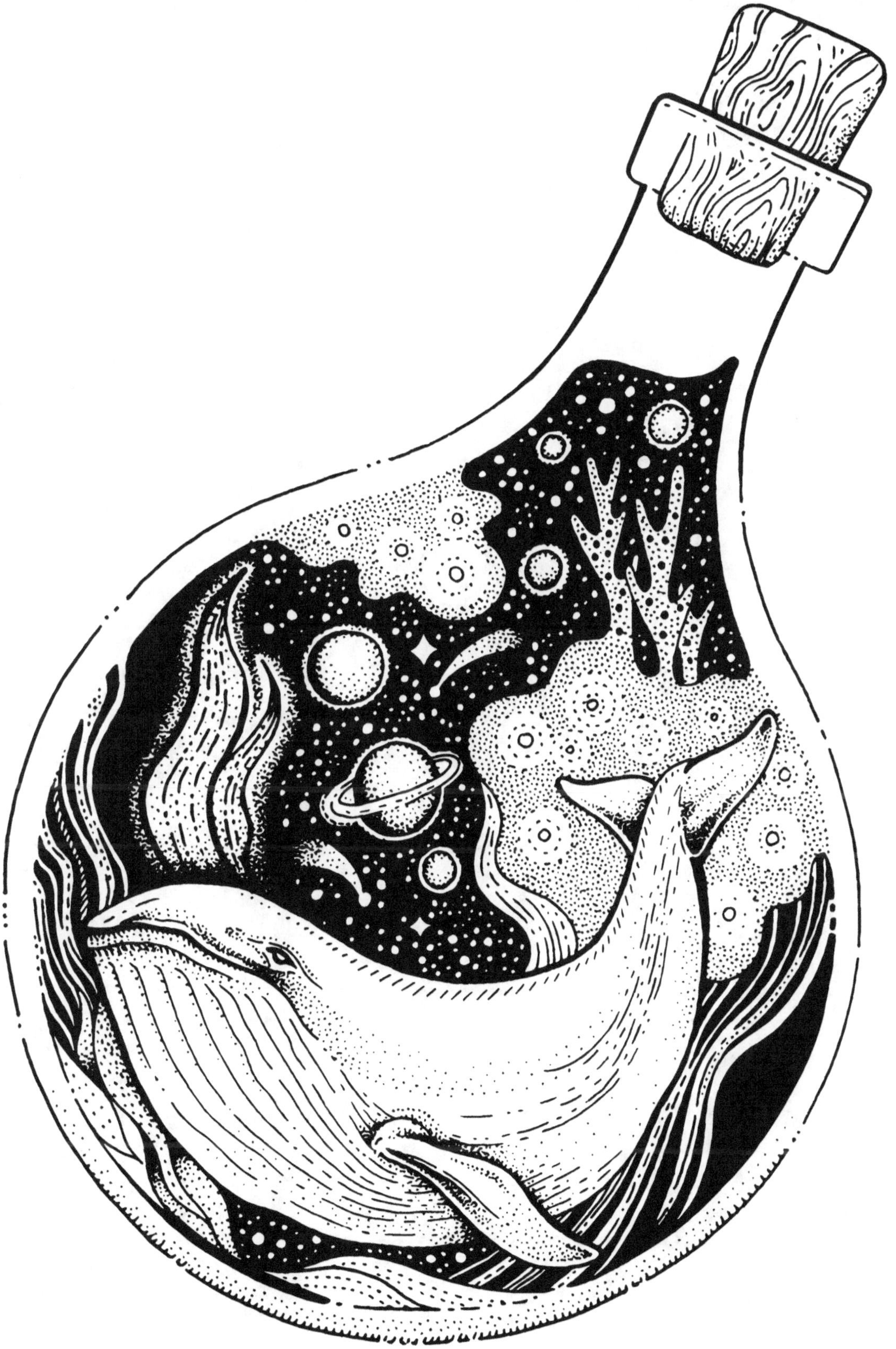

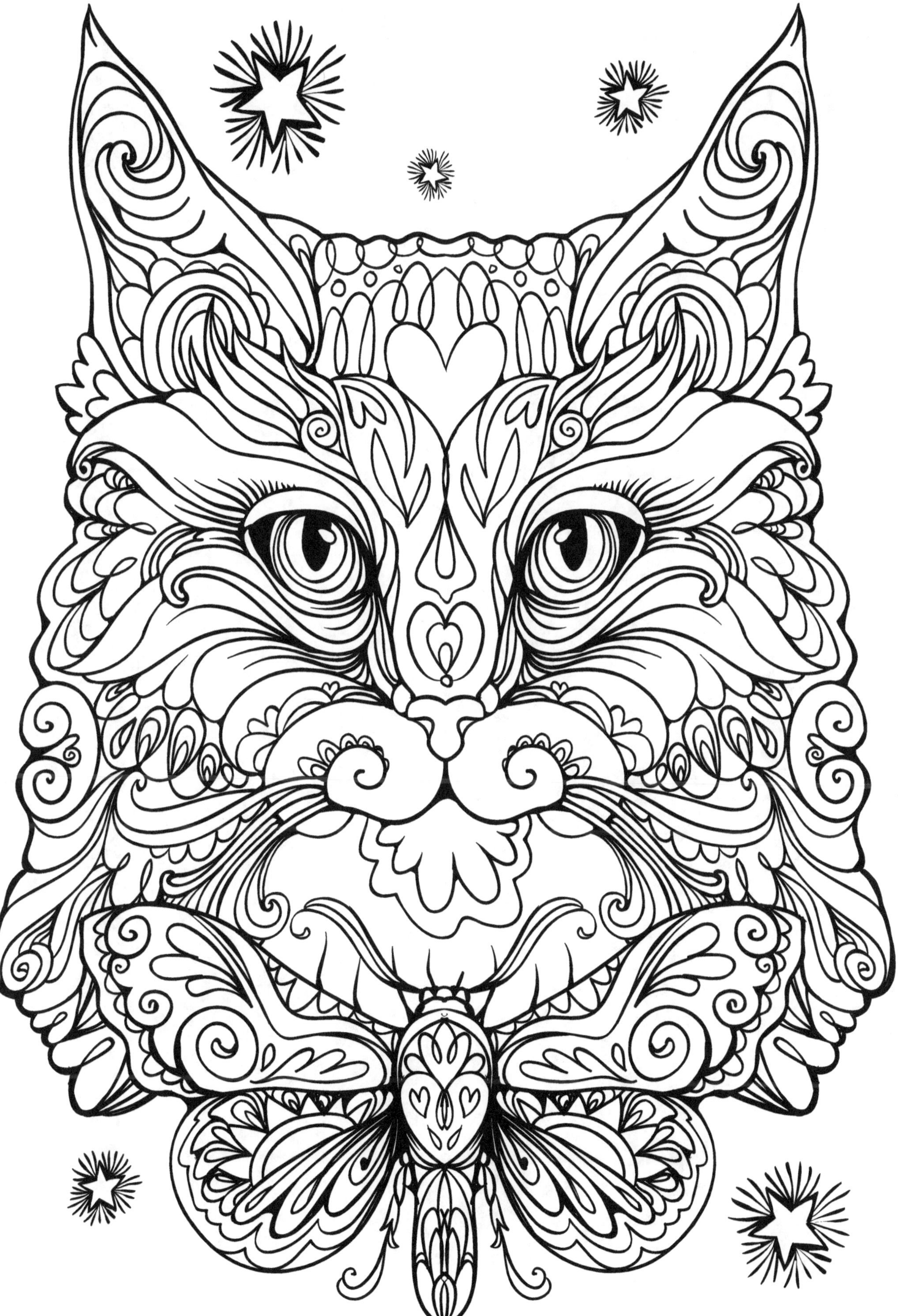

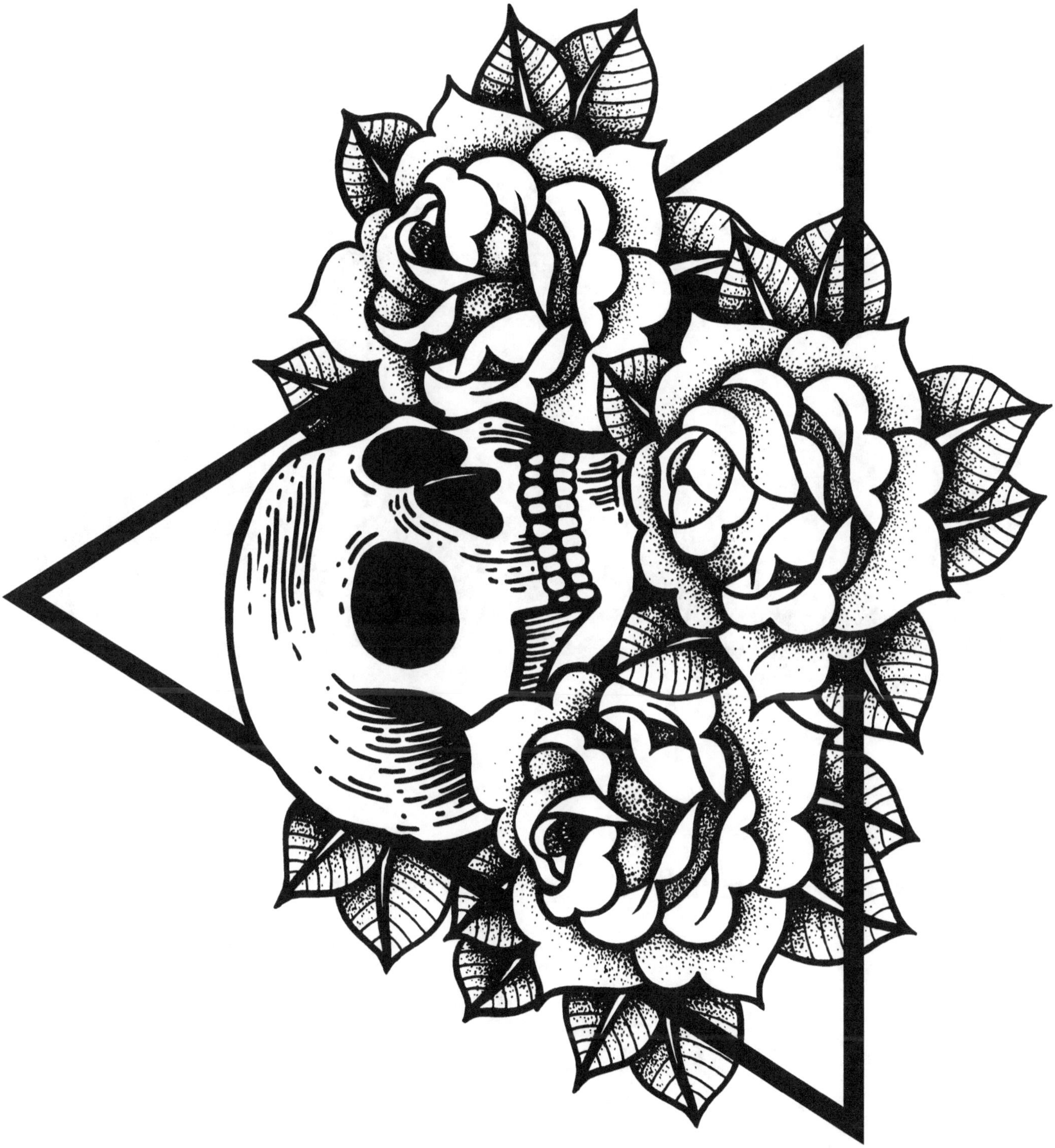

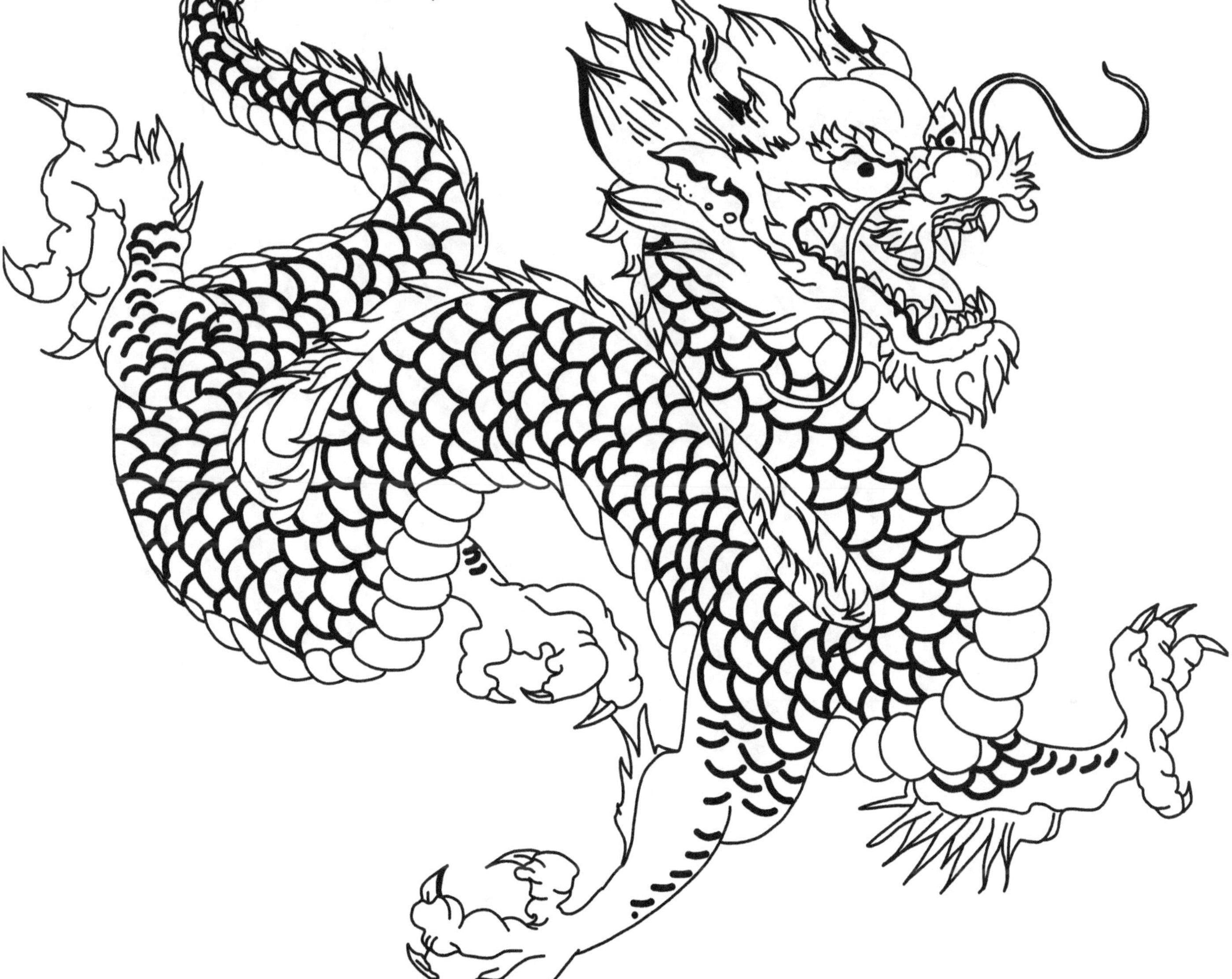

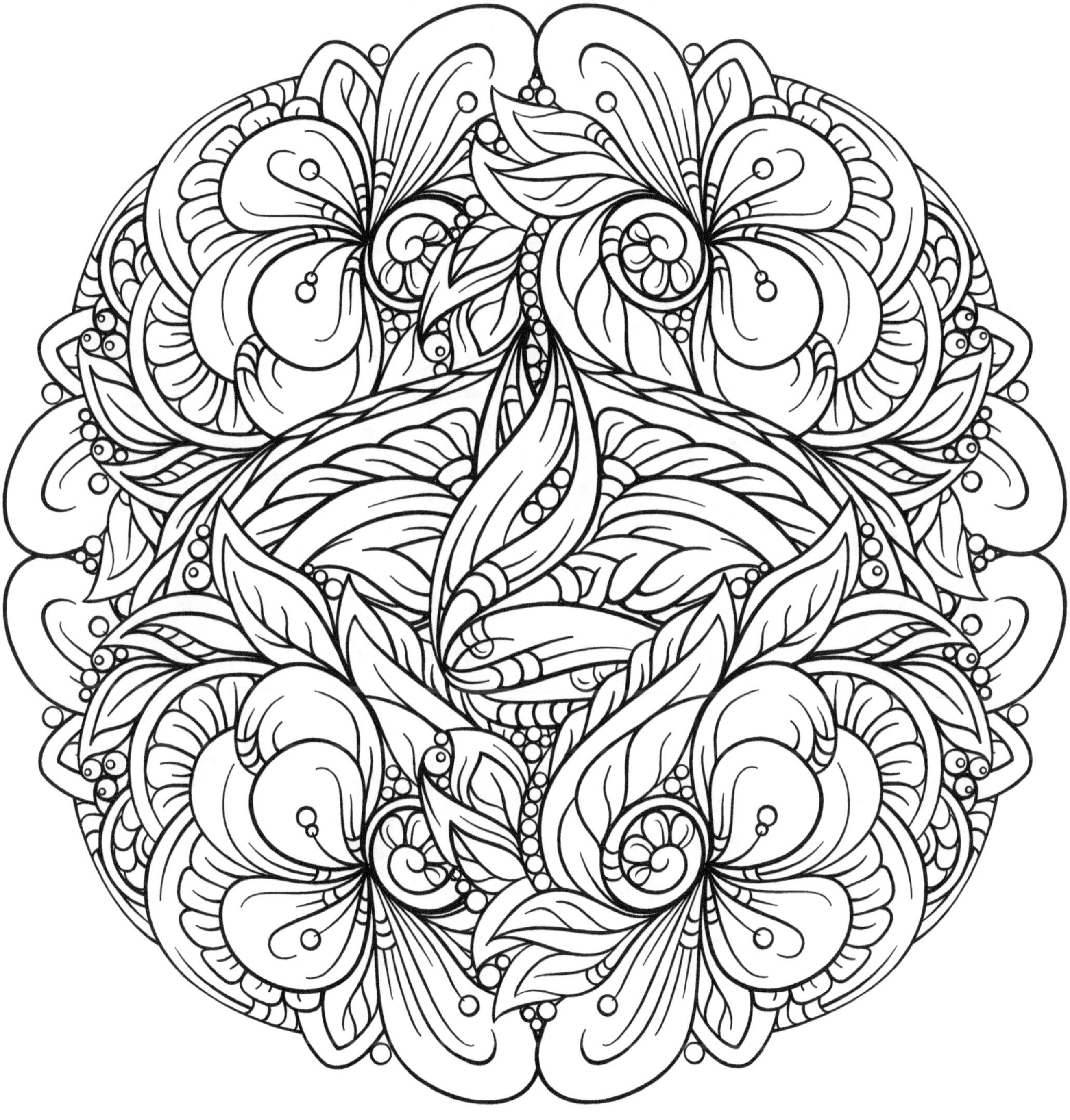

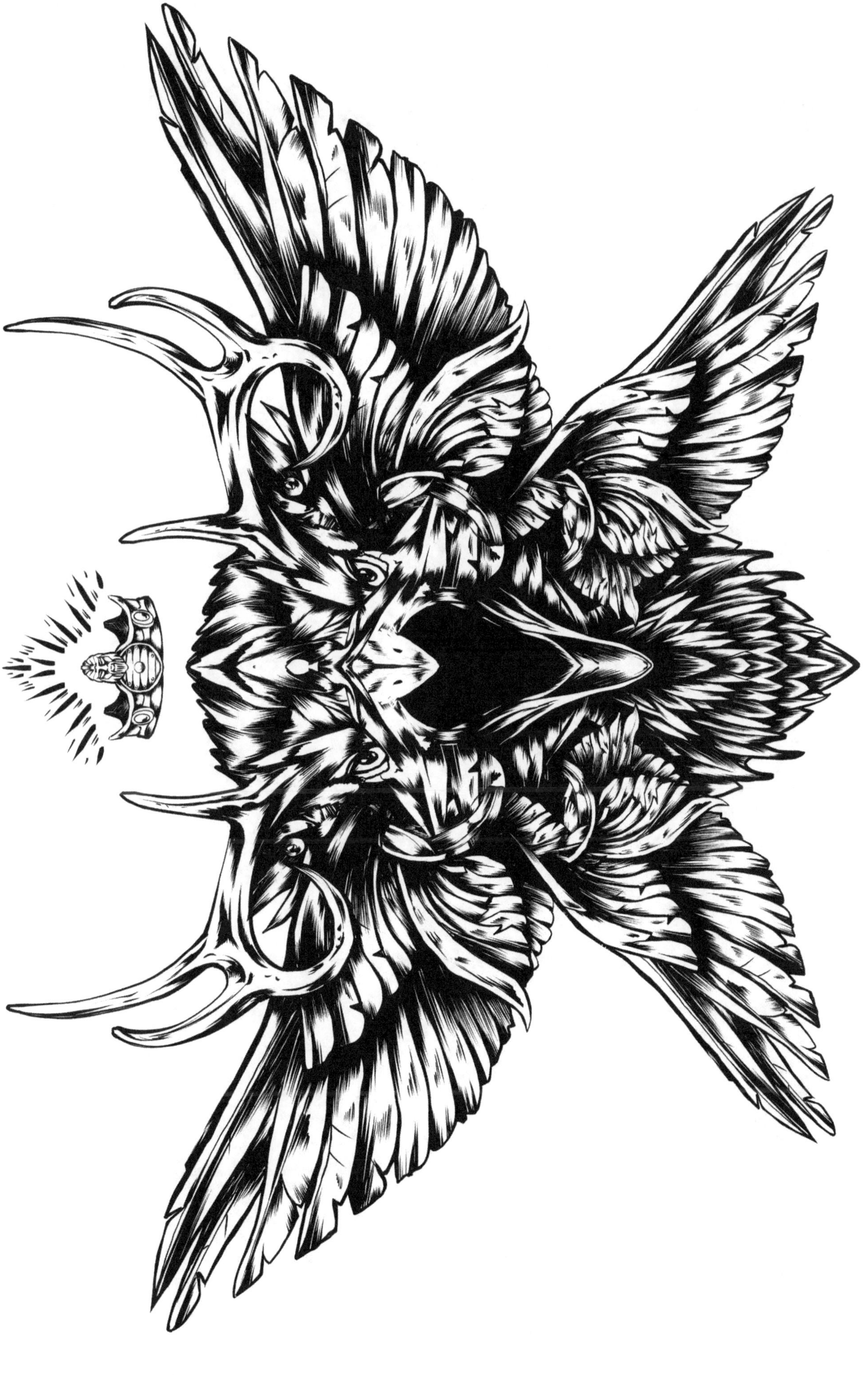

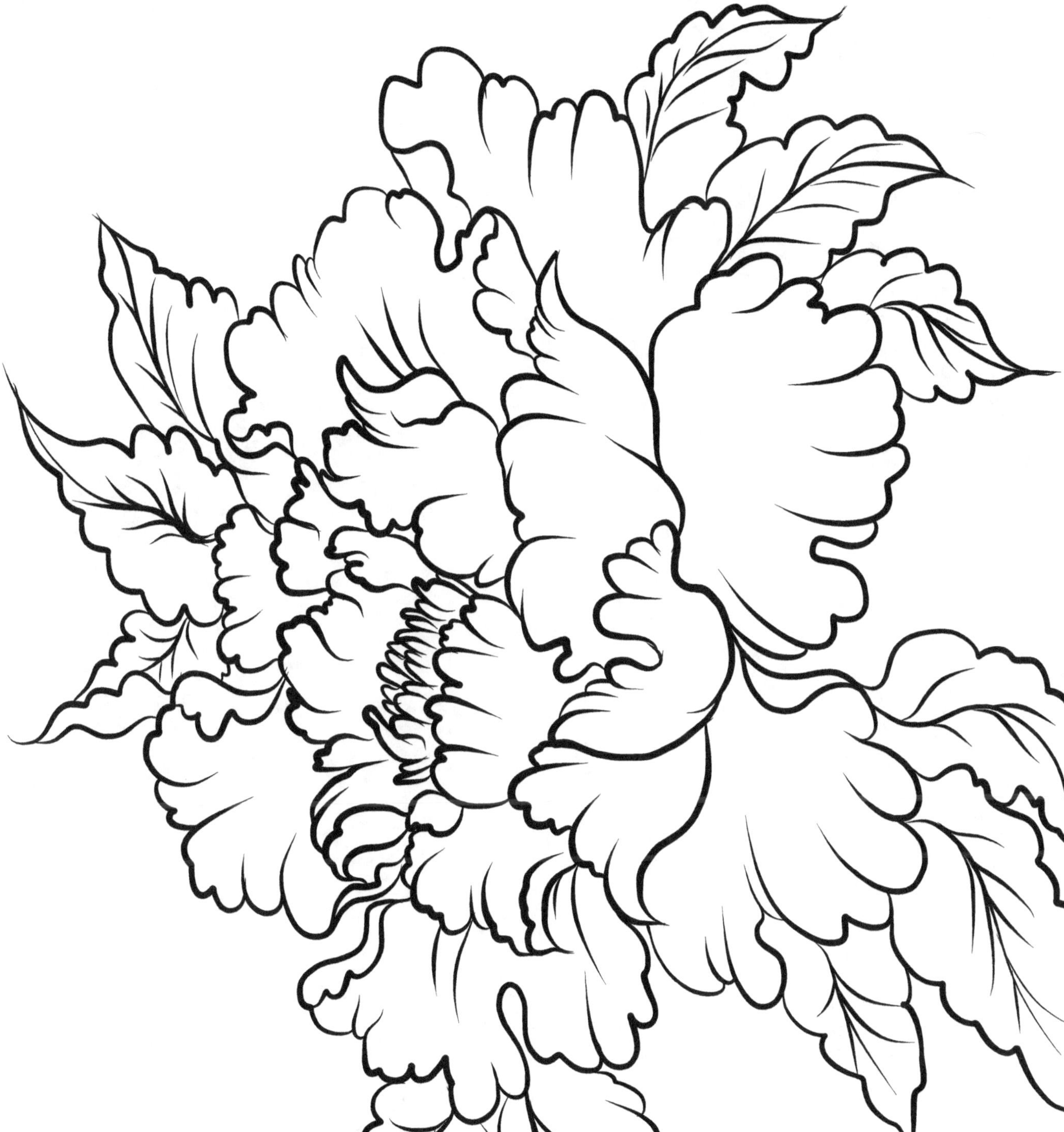

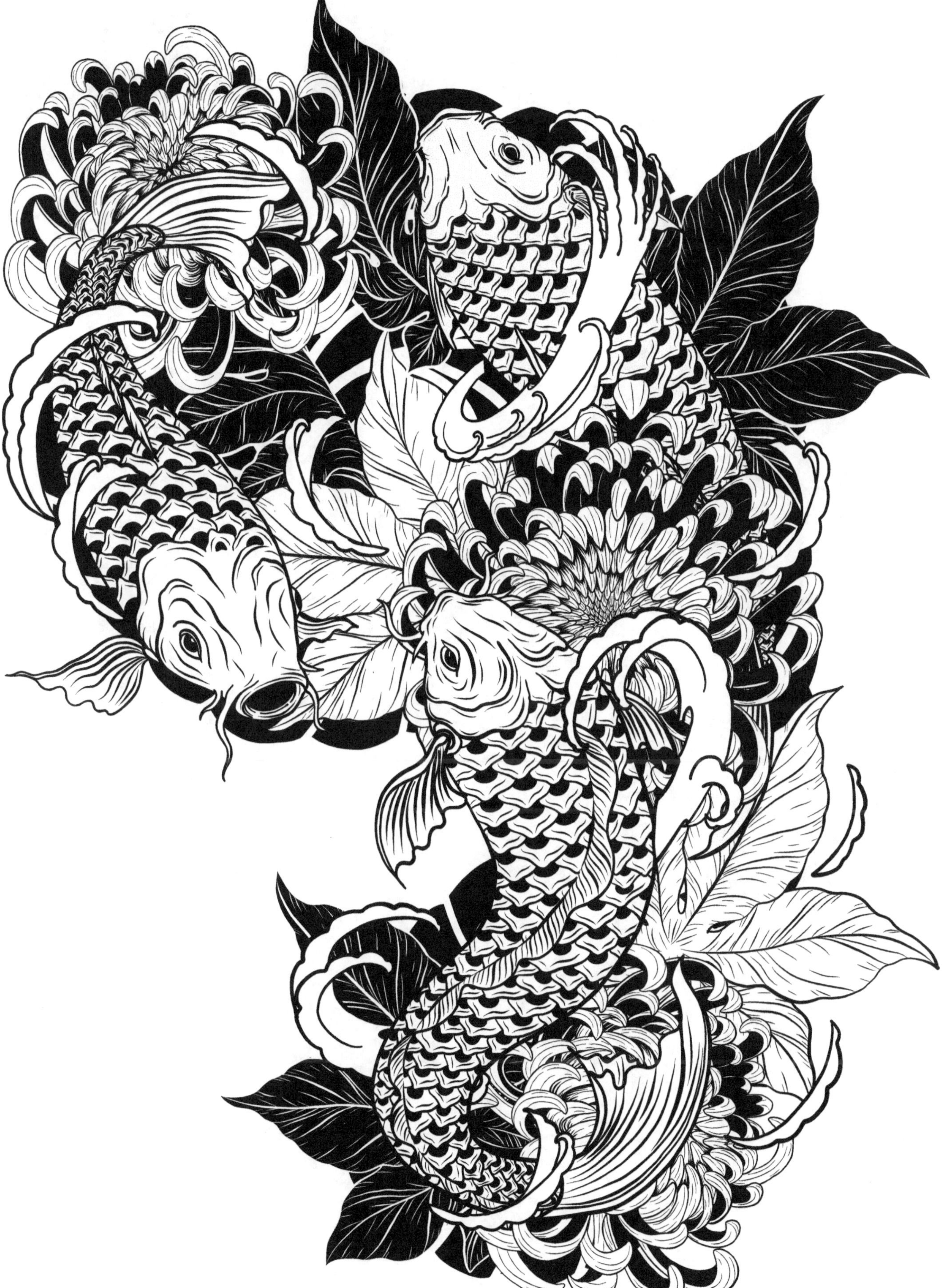

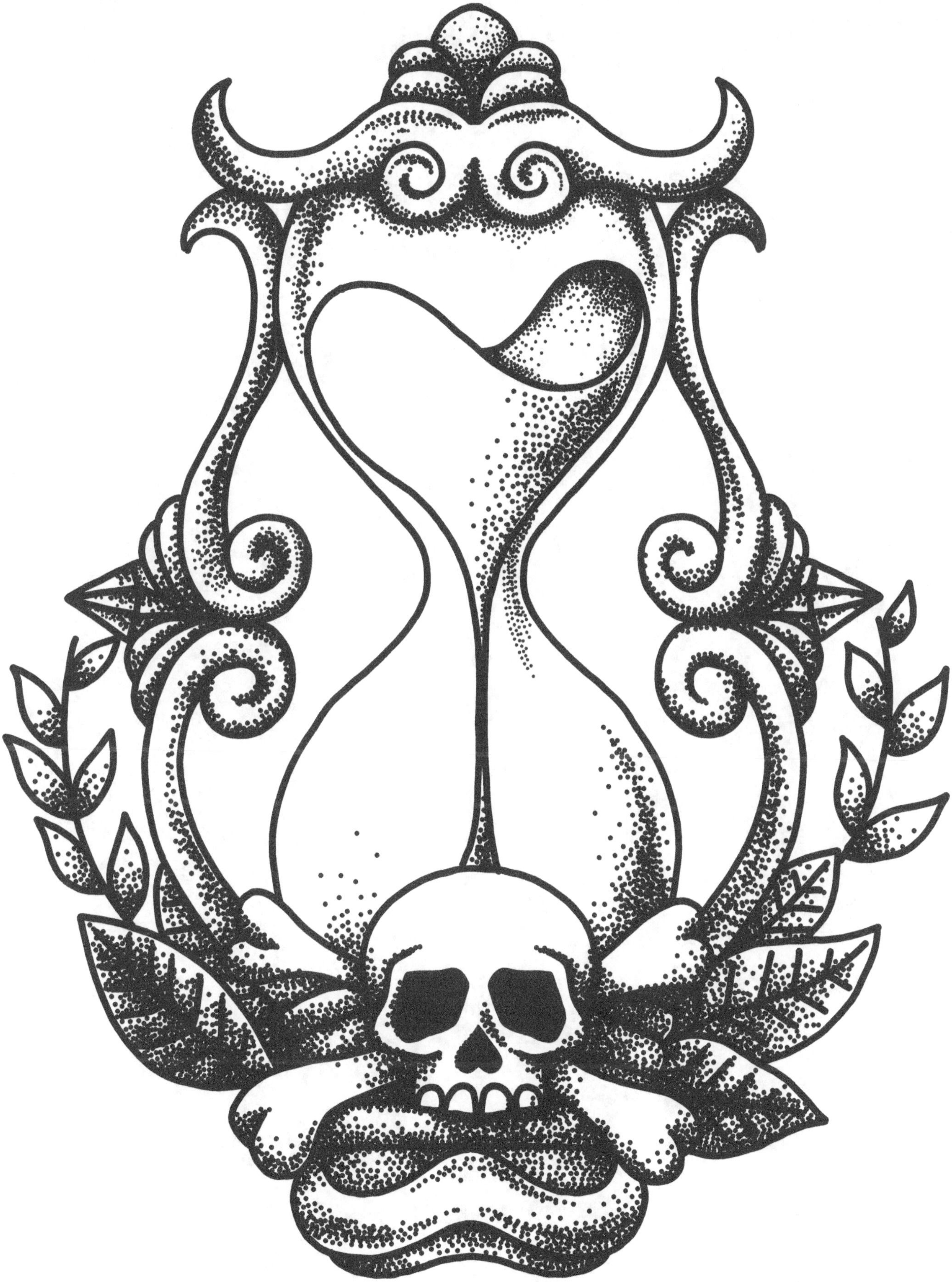

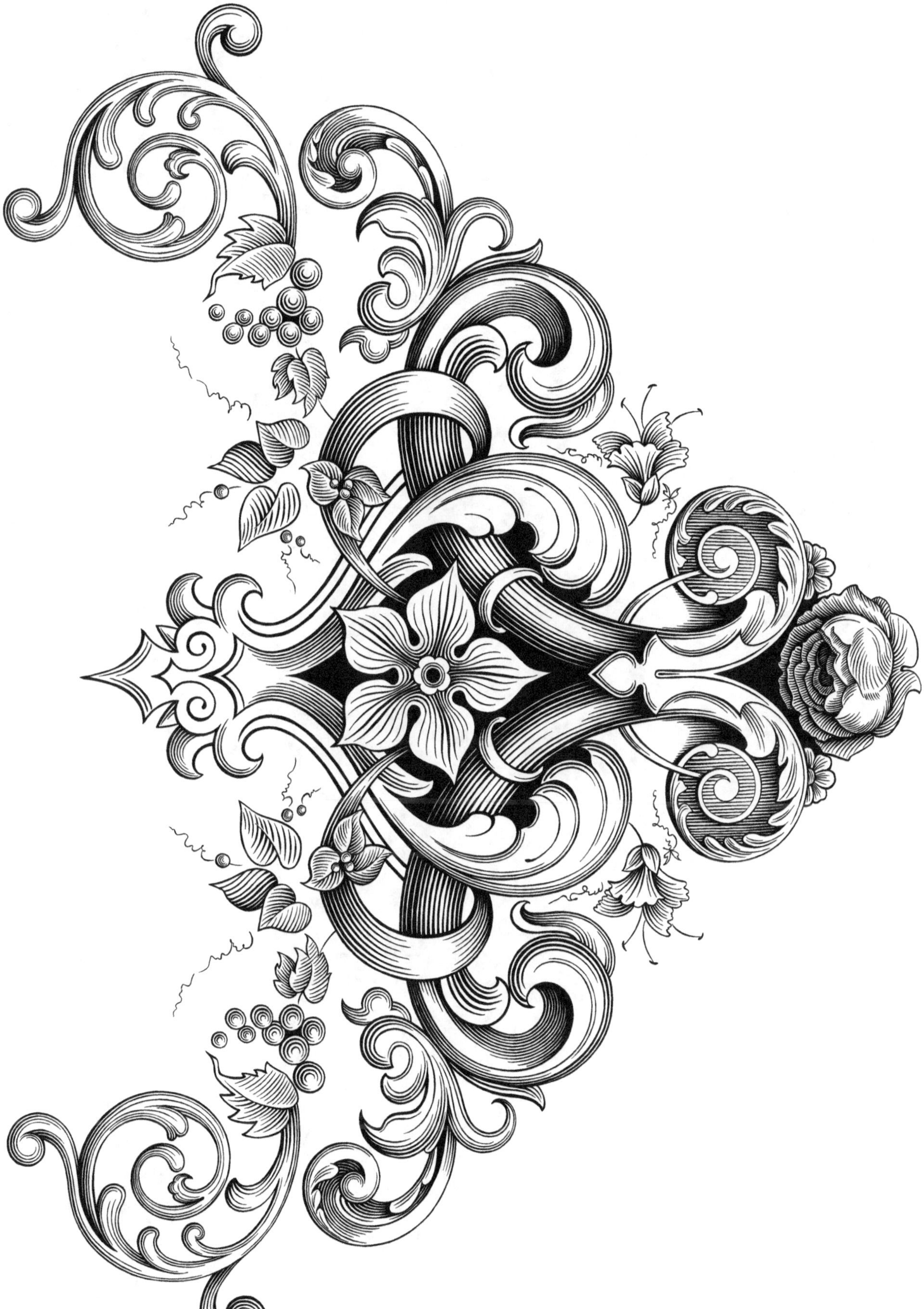

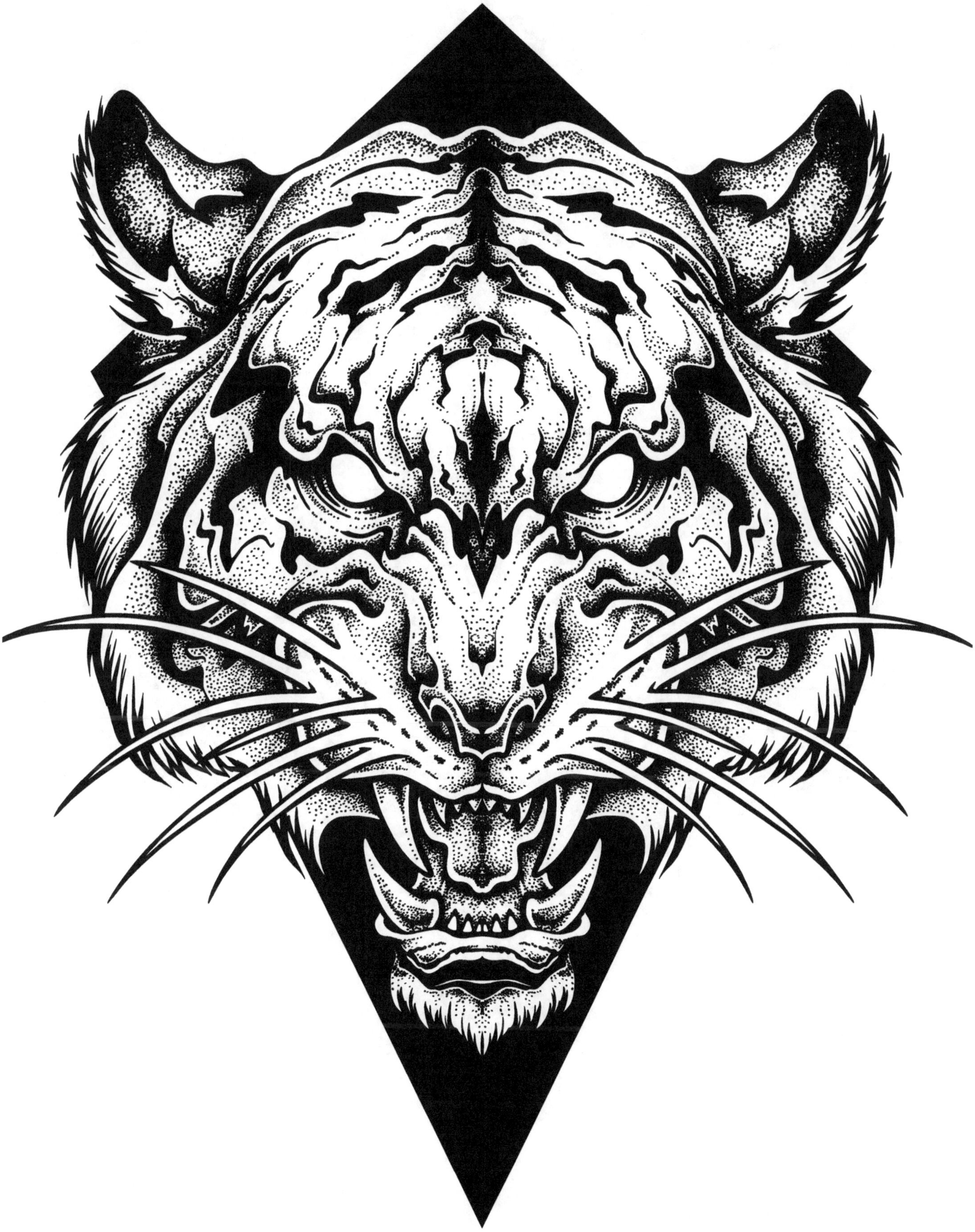

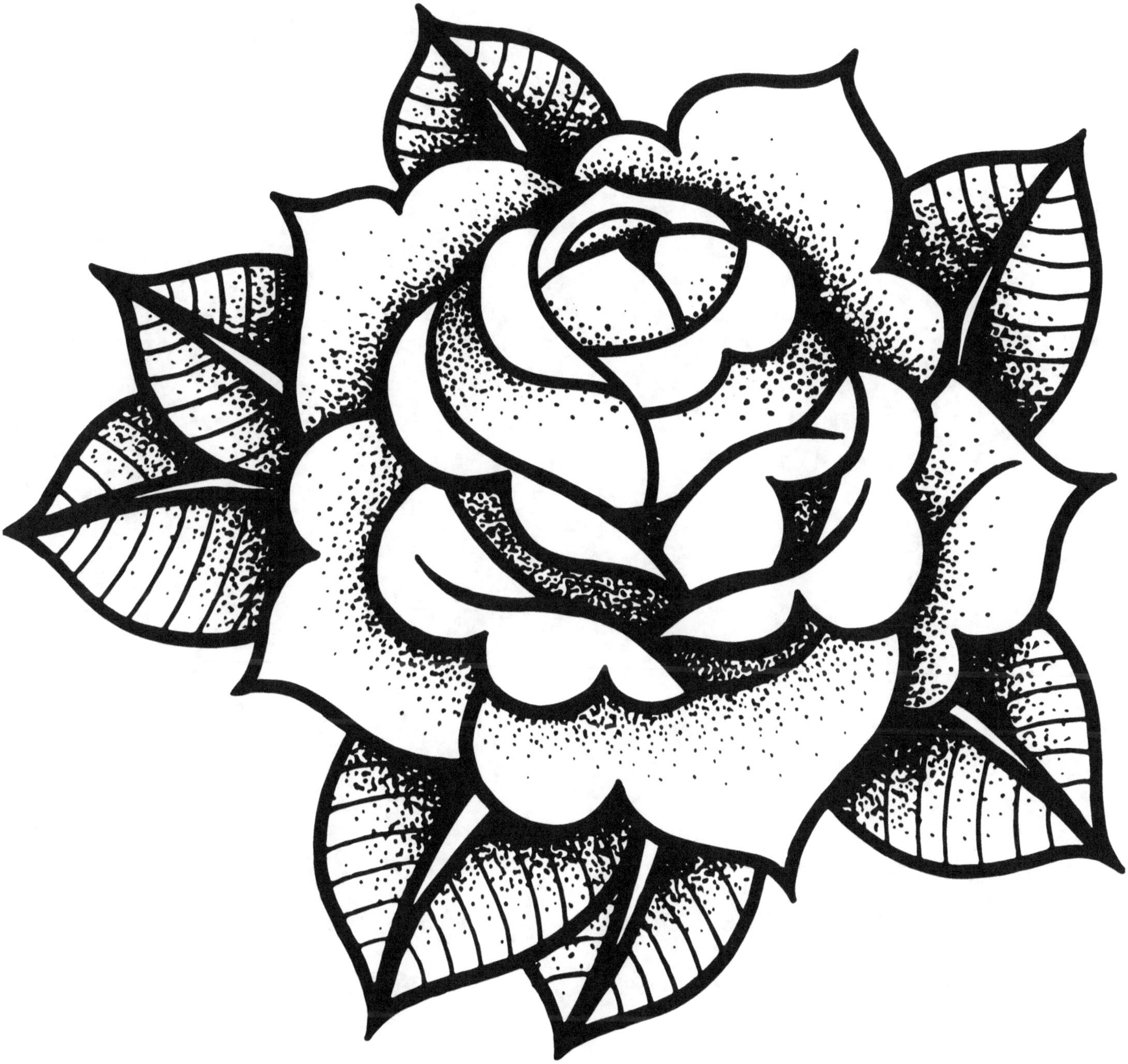

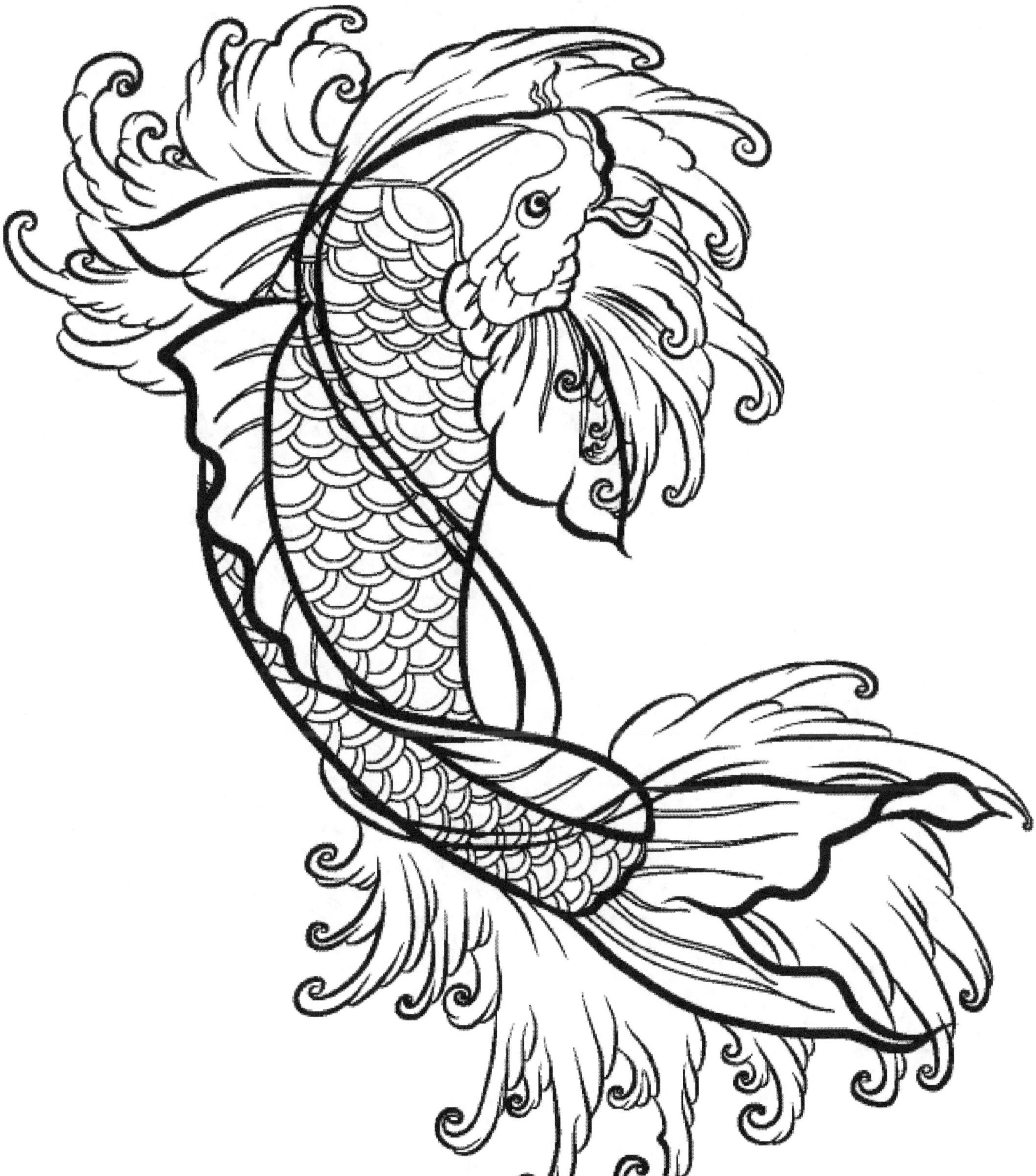

www.ingramcontent.com/pod-product-compliance
Lightning Source LLC
Chambersburg PA
CBHW081005170526
45158CB00010B/2911
* 9 7 8 1 0 8 2 0 0 8 2 3 8 *